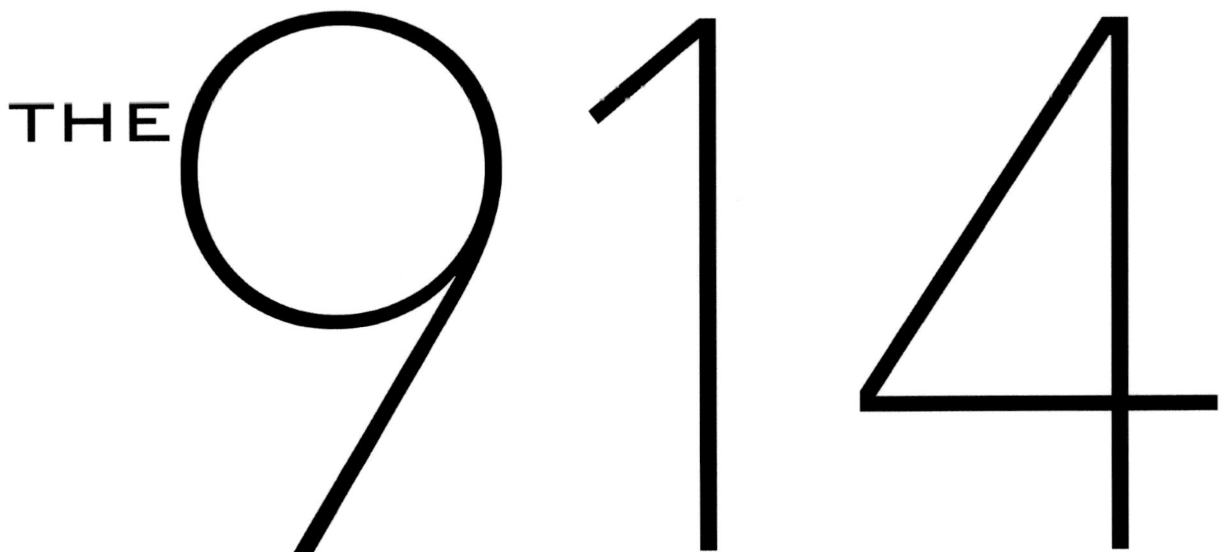

AND 914-6 PORSCHE

A Restorer's Guide To Authenticity III

Dr. B. Johnson
with
George Hussey

ISBN 0-929758-29-3 (978-0-929758-29-9)

Published by Beeman Jorgensen, Inc.,
7510 Allisonville Road, Suite 29, Indianapolis, Indiana 46250 U.S.A.

Printed and bound in the United States of America
Cover design by Llew Kinst, Cupertino, California
Cover photography by Julie Johnson and Hilde Mia Dejonckheere

Third Printing, February 2025

Contents

Acknowledgments

I would like to make special recognition of the assistance and photos I have received through the years from representatives of Porsche AG, including: Klaus Parr, Olaf Lang, Jens Torner, Tobias Mauler and most recently Frank Jung. In addition, I have been treated very well by folks at Porsche Cars North America including: Brad Ripley, Howard Adams and Wayne Stone. Without their help, this would be a much thinner and less accurate work.

Thanks to the following people for sharing their technical expertise and reviewing this text for accuracy: George Hussey, Automobile Atlanta; Mark Taylor, NLA Ltd.; Paul Domitrovic, Stoddard Parts; Dave Pateman, Jim Breazeale and Dr. Georg Konradsheim. Thanks also to Louise Haskett and Julie Johnson for their skilled editing.

Photos in this book are courtesy of 914 owners and enthusiasts including: Jim Bach, Dennis Brooks, Bill Calcagno, Hilde Mia Dejonckheere, Steve Gaglione, Thomas Gruber, TAG Books; George Hussey, Automobile Atlanta; Julie Johnson, Llew Kinst, Autograph Designed; Dr. Georg Konradsheim, Christoph Maeder, Bill Moore, A K Kissell, Arno Kissell, Scott Kuhne, Michael Ledwitz, Bill Lee, Stu Lehr, Pete Mayhew, Dom Miliano, Dave Pateman, David Siebert, Pete Simmons, Steve Stanislaus, Glenn Stazak, Gary Turner, John Wharton and Michael Wittke, Mittelmotor.

Brett Johnson
October 2020

My thanks to Phil Owings, my 914 mentor who first introduced me to the car by sliding me under one to repair it that long ago Saturday in August of 1974. While marveling at its engineering as compared to my MGB, from that day on I never looked back. And to my wife Mia, who's dedication to our business and hard hard work has made my 914 hobby a viable enterprise.

George Hussey
October 2020

Introduction

When the 914 Porsche was introduced to the world in 1969 it was met with mixed reviews. Its dual VW/Porsche personality in Europe and its obvious use of off-the-shelf VW components caused many enthusiasts to deny that it was enough Porsche to be a Porsche. These people were obviously not around in the early fifties when the only Porsches around had engines, gearboxes, wheels and interior components that also had a striking similarity to products from the cars produced in Wolfsburg. Despite the fact that many view the joint production and marketing as a less than successful endeavor, in its short seven-year existence nearly 117,000 were produced. This is almost twice the number of the total 356 Porsche production from 1950 through 1965.

Introduced at $3595, the 914 was an *entry level Porsche*, designed to leave the owner wanting more (more like a 911). As such, and due to the fact that there was certainly room for improvement, many examples of the model frequently changed hands. Since so many mechanical aspects of the car were provided by Volkswagen, aftermarket performance and cosmetic accessories developed for use on VWs were often installed.

One of the most frustrating parts of research has been locating original, unmodified cars for photography. Many well meaning former owners have altered cars, nearly beyond recognition in some cases. Restoring these to their original appearance is often the goal of a new owner, and for many it is not an easy task. Most answers are buried deep within the weighty, burgundy covered parts manuals that may still grace the shelves at the Porsche dealership. Other answers are seemingly lost to obscurity. While changes to the 900 series Porsches are more organized than those on the earlier 356 models, there are still some unacknowledged differences and running changes. In a number of cases Porsche superseded an original item with a superior piece. The result, while frustrating to the restorer, was meant to better the marque. We have attempted to bring some of these to light and also to illustrate the original part, where possible.

The purpose of this text is to aid those enthusiasts who wish to purchase a 914 or have taken on the restoration challenge, as well as to entertain the Porsche trivia buff. While there may be minor inaccuracies and uncertainties, we have attempted to put together a complete and accurate description of 1970 through 1976 Porsche 914 and 914-6 cars. It is our hope that those who can shed additional light on the information that follows will step forward and share it, so that it may be included in subsequent editions. Regardless, we feel that the information within will be helpful to the amateur, as well as the expert. We have tried to depict it in a logical, front to back, system-by-system, presentation of standard production vehicles. Subject matter now includes chassis, body, exterior trim, luggage compartments and interior with new chapters about engine and other mechanical systems. Reference material is contained in the final section.

We are in debt to those who supplied information and to those who have taken time to review this text for accuracy and to those who have provided images. In cases where non-original parts are found on photo subjects, we have endeavored to call them to the reader's attention. Thanks to changes in technology this third edition now has color images. In addition, online access is available to higher resolution versions of the photos contained within this book. Information about this service can be found at: www.tpr-inc.com

At the time of this writing the 914 Porsche, now celebrating its 50th anniversary, is recognized as a collectible automobile. Good original cars of any type are always desirable, but with the number of modified 914s that exist, authentic examples will always command premium prices, with the six-cylinder variety often exceeding six figures. The 914, Porsche's ugly duckling has become a swan and is finally accepted for its true value and position in Porsche history.

Brett Johnson
George Hussey
October 2020

Background

This book will examine the standard production versions of the Porsche 914 and 914-6. Where possible, comparison of the two exotic fourteeners, the 914-6 GT and 916, has been included.

For those not familiar with the 914's development, what follows is a thumbnail sketch (for greater detail I would recommend *Porsche, Excellence was Expected* by Karl Ludvigsen). Initially the 914 was designed as a car that would incorporate the new Volkswagen 411 engine and numerous mechanical components from other Volkswagen models. The resulting car was to be marketed by Volkswagen as a replacement for the aging Karmann Ghia. Porsche would also have the option of using their own mechanical components and marketing their own 914 version. Bodies were produced by Karmann, a company with strong historical ties to both Volkswagen and Porsche.

The final production arrangement for the introduction in late 1969 saw the 914 and 914-6 marketed in Europe through a joint venture of Volkswagen and Porsche as *VW-Porsches*. The thought behind the VW-Porsche name was to strengthen Volkswagen's image, but instead, the 914 and more so the 914-6 suffered from the mixed parentage, because they were considered by the car-buying public as something less than a Porsche, rather than more than a Volkswagen. Only in the United States and Canada were 914s sold through Porsche dealers as Porsche automobiles. Since Volkswagen of America had a separate Porsche-Audi division for distribution, dealers were able to convince VW that this strategy was appropriate. Indeed, the US market was one of the few to embrace the 914; as a result, nearly three-quarters of 914s were sold in the US and Canada. Throughout this text, these 914s will be referred to as US spec. Others will be referred to as either Euro spec. or RoW (Rest of World).

While there was only one body style, a number of engine types combined with varying trim combinations make restoration of the 914 or 914-6 a bit confusing. Record keeping by the Porsche factory was, all in all, much better than it was during earlier times, but there are still areas where information is sketchy. Unless stated otherwise, throughout this text the model year will be used to identify cars and features. In most cases the model year commenced in August of the preceding calendar year.

A general description of the various models of 914 and 914-6 is found on the pages following the section about Porsche part numbers. There is also a *Spotter's Guide* which allows identification of all years and models at a glance. It is found on pages 114-117.

The 914 Lineage

1970	1971	1972	1973	1974	1975	1976
914-6	914-6	914-6				
	914-6 GT	916	914 2.0	914 2.0	914 2.0	914 2.0
914-4	914-4	914-4	914 1.7	914 1.8	914 1.8	

Porsche Part Numbers

Those who have ventured into the local Porsche dealership on occasion are no doubt aware of the eleven-digit Porsche part number that identifies the components that make up each car. With the VW/Porsche split personality of the 914, quite a few nine digit numbers are present. These are VW numbers and they may or may not be followed by an alphabetic letter. While the numbers may be somewhat overwhelming by their sheer size, there is a logic to the format. A few general features will help both the novice and the expert.

The first group of three numbers generally relates to the car type or model for which the part was originally designed, engine type or gearbox type. Examples of Porsche numbers:

901	Early 911 or originally early 911
905	Sportomatic gearbox and associated hardware
911	Generally, 911 parts developed after 1969
914	914 specific parts

There are other numbers scattered throughout, including 904, 916, 917 and 930. These imply origin in the development of other Porsche projects. There are even 616s which are holdovers from the 356.

900 and 999 begin part numbers fitting the general classification of hardware, i.e. nuts, bolts etc. It appears that 999 tends to be more of a standard *off the shelf* component, while 900 represents a more specialized part.

VW numbers are similar. Those numbers starting with 1, such as 111, 113, and 141 relate to the Beetle (Type 1). The 2s, such as 211 have Bus/Transporter (Type 2) origins. The 3s, such as 311, 321 and 341 are derived from the Squareback/Fastback (Type 3) models. 411, 473 and other 4s relate to the ill-fated 411/412 (Type 4). There are also some 8 numbers. These have Audi ancestry.

Numbers starting with 0 are mechanical, often engine parts. As a rule 021 relates to 1.7 liter engines, 022 to 1.8s and 039 to 2.0s. This is not a one hundred percent rule, so exercise care when ordering mechanical components.

The final variety of VW numbers are those that start with *N*. These correspond to the Porsche 900s and 999s, which are hardware. These *N numbers* do not follow the standard format. Their first grouping has either two or three numbers, the middle group always three and the final group one or two.

The second group of three in both Porsche and VW part numbers serves to further define the part. For example, in the number 914.559.459.10, which is a 1.8 script, and 914.559.257.10, which is a left horn grille, the 559 is a number which defines insignias and other trim parts.

In the part number above, the third group (257) is used to define side. Nearly all left (driver's) side parts end in odd numbers and are generally lower numerically than their right counterpart. Conversely, all right numbers are even and generally higher than their left counterpart. In this case, the corresponding right horn grille is a 911.559.258.10. If the part is not sided, it will be odd. Since the 914 engine was originally positioned in the opposite direction from its VW of origin, most sided items from the engine are opposite to the convention discussed above.

The final pair of numbers again further defines the part. It was a little clearer cut in the 356 series of numbering: for the most part, 00 represented the first permutation of a part with higher numbers such as 01, 02 etc. being subsequent modifications. Unfortunately, this is not always the case with the 914. The 1.8 script part number 914.559.459.10 was actually the first, not the tenth version of this script.

Throughout the text, part numbers will be referenced when it seems appropriate, but not in an attempt to overwhelm the reader nor add to the page count by listing them for each part described.

Reference Materials

Aside from actual examples of the marque, input from their owners and a little personal experience, most of the information contained within came from carefully researching the factory parts manuals and microfiche.

Other relevant publications used as references, included factory color books, sales literature, option lists, owner's manuals, accessories catalogs and the chassis number chart found in George Hussey's *914 Tech Tips 700*.

The Models

Corporate Archives Porsche AG

914-4, 1970-72

The first of the four-cylinder cars were known by the 914-4 designation. They used the modified 1.7 liter Volkswagen 411 engine. Chrome bumpers and vinyl-covered rear roof pillars were part of the optional appearance group (*additional details, page 121*). These panels were painted the body color on standard trim 914-4s.

Standard 4½ x 15" wheels were silver-painted Volkswagen rims with plain chrome hub caps. Non-US cars had VW emblems on the hub caps. Wider 5½ x 15" alloy wheels made by Pedrini were optional.

The interior of the 914-4 was stark at best. In 1970 and 1971 the passenger's seat was not adjustable. Instead, a curious tethered footrest was installed. This attempt to save manufacturing cost was corrected in 1972 when conventional seats on sliding rails were used on both sides.

MOTOR TREND
Import Car of the Year

914 1.7, 914S, 914 2.0, 1973

In 1973 the 1.7 engine was standard and a 2.0 liter engine was offered as an option, thus it became necessary to differentiate the two with the scripts on the tail panel. The 2.0 was originally called the 914S by the US importer. This was not well received by Porsche AG, so the *1.7* and *2.0* numbers were adopted officially. The 914S name did stick in the UK, though.

Black bumpers replaced body color ones with the standard trim package. Chrome bumpers and upholstered roof pillars were again offered in the appearance group option package (*additional details, page 121*). US cars had rubber bumper guards up front.

Standard wheels were the steel Volkswagen ones used on the 914-4. Optional wheels, all 5½ x 15", included a steel wheel, the Pedrini and Mahle cast alloy wheels, and the Fuchs four-spoke forged alloy wheel.

The interior of the 2.0 featured an optional center console fitted with additional instruments.

914 1.8, 2.0, Limited Edition, 1974

The displacement of the smaller engine was increased from 1679cc to 1795cc, although due to emission controls in North America, power was lower. The 2.0 remained unchanged.

Rubber bumper guards were now present front and rear on US specification cars. Vinyl covering on the roof pillars was standard on all models except the Limited Edition.

The Limited Edition model was produced from mid-February through early-April 1974. It was a 2.0 with a special front spoiler available in two color choices. The bumpers, valances, rocker panels and wheel centers were painted yellow (black exteriors) or orange (white exteriors). They also featured Mahle wheels with painted centers, sway bars, driving lights and upgraded interior appointments including center console, map box and foam steering wheel (*details on page 121*).

The appearance group no longer featured chrome bumpers, but still had interior and exterior appointments listed on page 121.The standard steel wheels were now 5½ x 15" sport wheels. Cast Mahle and forged Fuchs alloy wheels were optional.

PORSCHE
914 2.0
74 CANAM

PORSCHE

914 1.8, 2.0, 1975-76

The same engine options were offered as in 1974. Power was the same for the 1.8, but was down seven horsepower (more in California) on the 2.0, due to the installation of an air pump.

The front and rear chassis structure was reinforced to accommodate the new rubber-covered, impact-absorbing bumpers mounted front and rear. Additional rubber guards were required in some US states. Optional fog/driving lights were rectangular. Wheel options were unchanged from 1974.

Interior changes were confined to different materials. A new wide pattern basket-weave vinyl and optional tartan cloth seat inserts set these final 914s apart from their predecessors.

737-EPX

914-6, 1970-72

The 2.0 liter six-cylinder engine set the 914-6 apart from its four-cylinder counterpart. The 110 horsepower output was identical to the 1968-1969 911T. A few 1970 and 1971 914-6s had Sportomatic transmissions.

There were few visual cues that the 914-6 was not a 914-4. All 914-6s had chrome bumpers and vinyl-covered rear roof pillars. A 914-6 on the tail panel and slightly different tail pipe location were the only external differences aside from the 911 wheels.

Steel 5½ x 15" 911 wheels were standard. Options included chrome plated steel wheels, cast Mahle 5½ x 15" alloy wheels and forged Fuchs 5½ x 14" alloy wheels.

Interior differences centered around instruments and controls. The six borrowed heavily from 911s in the way of engine, suspension and brakes, in contrast to the four which had Volkswagen components. There were also 911 sourced components among the interior controls. For the most part these reverted to VW items in the final year of production.

DB·9146

914-6 M471 Option Package, 1971-72

This option group was available from March 1971 through 1972. The differences from standard 914-6s included the following: steel flares on all four fenders, flared fiberglass or steel front valance, flared fiberglass rocker panels and generally no rear valance.

Wheels were 6 x 15" Fuchs forged alloys. 21 mm spacers were added to move the wheels outward. Longer wheel studs were also used.

TSQ-934
PORSCHE

916, 1972

This wolf-in-cheap-clothing was proposed for production in 1972, but only 11 such examples were built. A sole example was delivered to the US. To be attractive on the US market, it was felt that air conditioning needed to be offered; however, the air conditioning compressor limited travel of the driver's seat. This and the projected price of $12,000 - $14,000 (more than a 911S) for this 190 horsepower car apparently kept it from reaching fruition. Only 2.4 911/56 engines were originally fitted, though many were upgraded.

The steel, non-removable top and radio antenna imbedded in the windshield were unique features of the 916. The fiberglass front and rear bumper treatment was also considerably different than the run of the mill 914. Rocker panels were also fiberglass, but the flares on the fenders were steel. The rear grille was altered, allowing improved cooling. Wheels used on the 916 were forged Fuchs 7 x 15" alloys all around.

The interior was much better appointed than standard 914s. In some, unique paisley cloth inserts were used on the seats. Elsewhere leather predominated, from headliner to door panels to carpet edging.

914-6 GT, 1970-71

Built for competition, the two-liter 914-6 GT won the first IMSA race ever held and took class wins at Le Mans and other international events. The type of event and race sanctioning body dictated the mechanical equipment installed. Complicating what was and was not a GT is the fact that no specific run of chassis numbers (as with the 916) identifies them. In theory, any 914-6 could be made into a GT with one of the 400 GT kits that Porsche was happy to provide. Research indicates that there were 32 factory-built GTs. The street version M471 cars were included in lists for homologation purposes.

Both brakes and engines were adapted from 911 production cars and mixed with current Zuffenhausen racing equipment (e.g. the 908 front brake calipers). The rear chassis was braced with strengthening plates following lessons learned in early 1970 testing.

The body featured the same flared fenders and engine lid used on the 916. The rocker panels were flared at the ends and made from fiberglass. The fiberglass bumpers front and rear were one-piece units resembling the bumper and upper cap piece found on standard 914s. Front and rear lids were light-weight fiberglass with balsa wood strengthening members on the inside. The top, which bolted in place, had an inner metal framework and bolted to the roof pillars. Some cars featured Plexiglas side and rear windows.

Wheels came in different combinations depending on need, but were generally Fuchs forged alloys. The normal mix was 6s in the front with 7s in the rear or 7s in the front with 8s in the rear.

The interior was as stark as one would expect for a racing machine. Simple flat door panels with hand- pulled door release covered a standard window-lift mechanism. The lower dash area was felt-covered, omitting most of the standard upholstery.

2
S-W1948
DUNLOP
CIBIE
IODE

TOYOTA
40
SONAUTO
PORSCHE
105 BC 92

TRICO
PORSCHE | AUDI
KENDALL GT-1
59
CAMEL
CHAMPION
GOODYEAR

Chassis

Inner Nose and Luggage Compartment

The unit body construction of the 914 made most of its outer panels part of the chassis. Indeed, only the lids, doors and top were removable. For purposes of definition, external body parts will be listed in the following chapter with internal parts described here.

The inner nose panel was completely hidden by the bumper and valance. On the inside it held the lower part of the hood latch. The nose panel also formed the front of the boxes in which the headlights were located. The front panel remained the same until the 1973 model year when a semi-circular brace was added inside the trunk and the areas just inside the headlight boxes were widened. This was to reinforce the area where US bumper guards had been added to absorb front impacts. When the larger bumpers were added for the 1975 model year, the above-mentioned brace was deleted, the nose panel was strengthened and the headlight boxes shortened to accommodate the US version crash bumper shock absorbers.

The bottom of the 1970-1974 nose panel had nine holes with rubber plugs

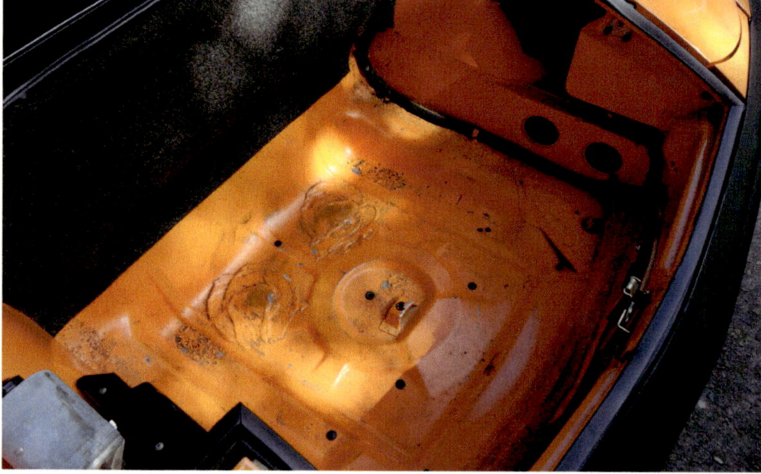

Inner nose area 1970-1972

The nose panel was modified for the 1975-1976 models for the impact absorbing bumpers. Holes at the bottom also disappeared

Semi-circular brace was added for US spec. cars in 1973-1974

1974 Japanese spec. Limited Edition without brace seen on US cars

Reworked inner nose with bumper shock absorbers from 1975-1976

The upper mount of the shock absorber in the strut type front suspension mounted to the inner front fender. On 914-6s, rubberized undercoating was applied to this area (and to selected other locations) following the installation of the front suspension. Undercoating was optional on four-cylinder cars.

For chassis rigidity, a brace of square tubing connected the left and right shock absorber mounts on the 914-6 GT when the larger GT fuel tank was installed (*see page 56*). In these car the front bulkhead was removed necessitating the brace.

Original undercoating on 914-6 upper shock absorber mount

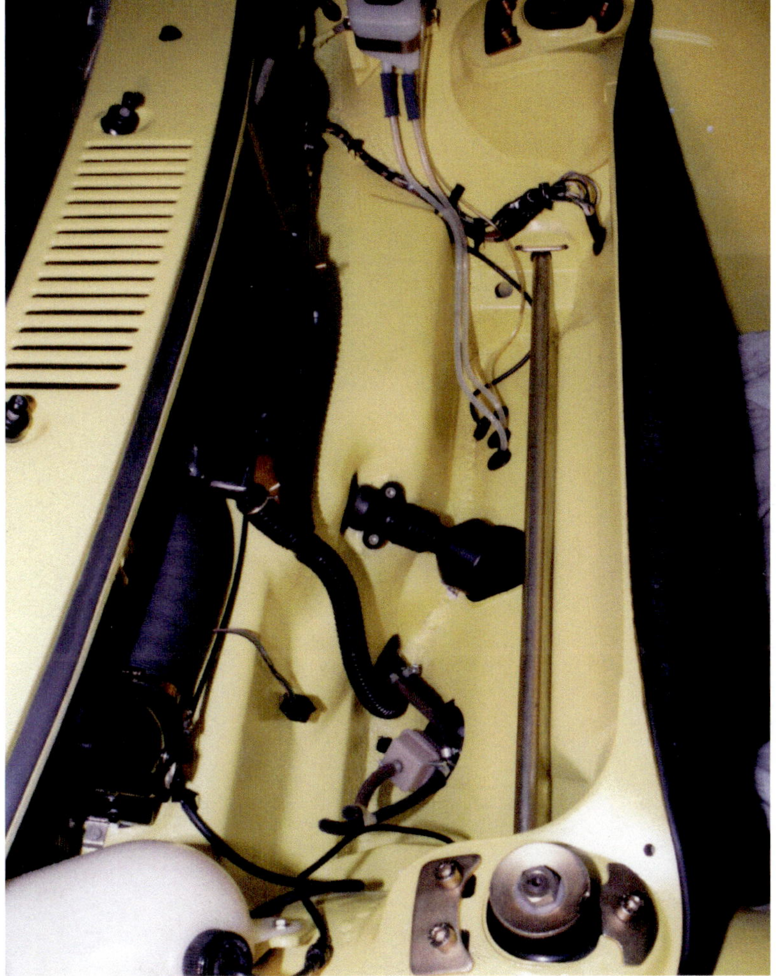

Optional anti-sway bar passed under the fuel tank in front of the steering shaft

The anti-sway bar, when fitted to 1972-1976 models, went through the luggage compartment below the fuel tank, penetrating a triangular bracket on each inner fender. No changes were made to these panels throughout production.

In the corners where the nose met the inner fender were the boxes holding the headlight units. Below each box was a short round tube

Installation of the GT tank necessitated removal of the front bulkhead and mounting a strut brace for chassis rigidity

Headlight box with headlight unit removed

Front chassis with tow hook 1976

which allowed water to drain. The boxes were shortened and the tubes lengthened to accommodate the bumper shocks in 1975. Through 1974 the manufacturer's identification plate was attached to the right side headlight box.

Below the light box was a longitudinal structural element. On US cars this panel was modified for 1973 and again for 1975. These resulted from changes in bumper regulations.

Forming the bottom of the luggage compartment was a floor section continuing from the nose panel to the rear of the passenger compartment. The front suspension was attached to the underside as was the

Early longer headlight box with I.D. plate, 1970-1974

Air conditioner condenser 1974 Limited Edition

towing hook. This hook was altered and lowered for the 1974 models. The only other change in this part occurred when the front bumper was modified in 1975. US cars fitted with dealer installed air conditioning had a large rectangular section of the floor cut away so the condenser could be installed.

Between the front luggage compartment and the fuel tank area was a steel partition. In 1975 the fuel pump was relocated to a compartment at the left lower part of the partition. Also at this time, the manufacturer's identification plate was moved from the right headlight box to the upper right of this panel.

Shorter headlight box to accommodate bumper shocks 1975-1976

1975-1976 relocated I.D. plate and fuel pump (lower right)

Stamped chassis number and octane sticker on top of the right wheel house

The chassis number was also stamped on top of the chassis which covered the right front wheel area. To the inside of this was a sticker with information about minimum gasoline octane requirements.

Driver's Compartment

With the exception of the addition of seat rails in 1972, the floor of the driver's compartment was not modified. Welded to the floor was a central tunnel which housed the shift linkage, clutch and accelerator cables, brake line, fuel line and wiring. The seat belt bolt receivers were relocated to the tunnel and bolt cages modified January 1, 1972, when retractable-style seat belts were added. A second modification occurred in 1973, when the gearshift linkage was redesigned.

Outer rocker panel removal reveals the structural inner rocker and jack receiver

A corresponding change was made to the lower bulkhead (*illustration 8/2, number 12*) at the rear of the driver's compartment to accommodate the smaller shift bushing and the corresponding shift cover.

The outer chassis box section or threshold area was made from four components: the longitudinal members (*illustration 8/1/1, number 1*) threshold panels, inner rocker panels (*illustration 8/2, numbers 19 and 18*) and inner wheel houses. Within the box was a two-piece conduit with muffler, which suppressed engine noise, that carried the heat to the driver's compartment.

The inner rocker and threshold panels (*illustration 8/2, numbers 18 and 19*) ran the length of the door. At the back of the inner rocker

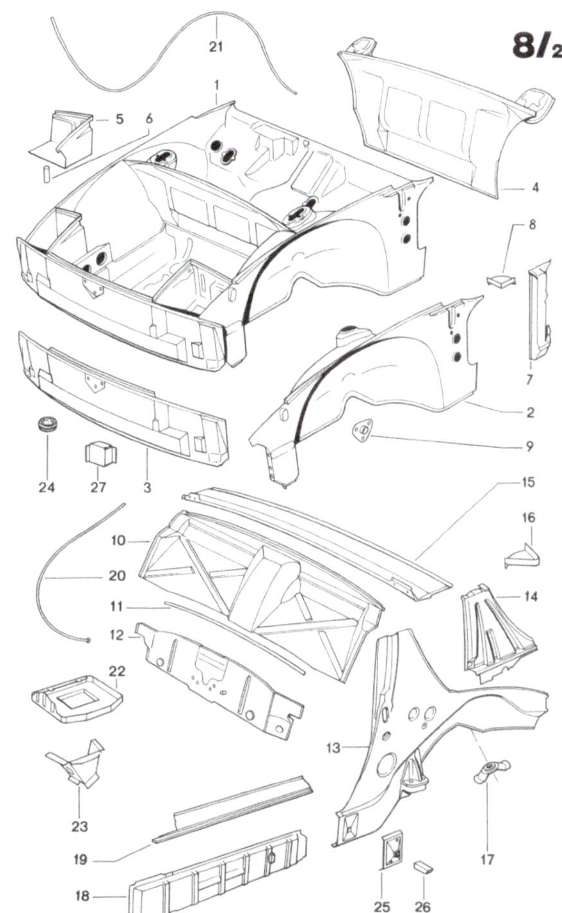

Illustration 8/2

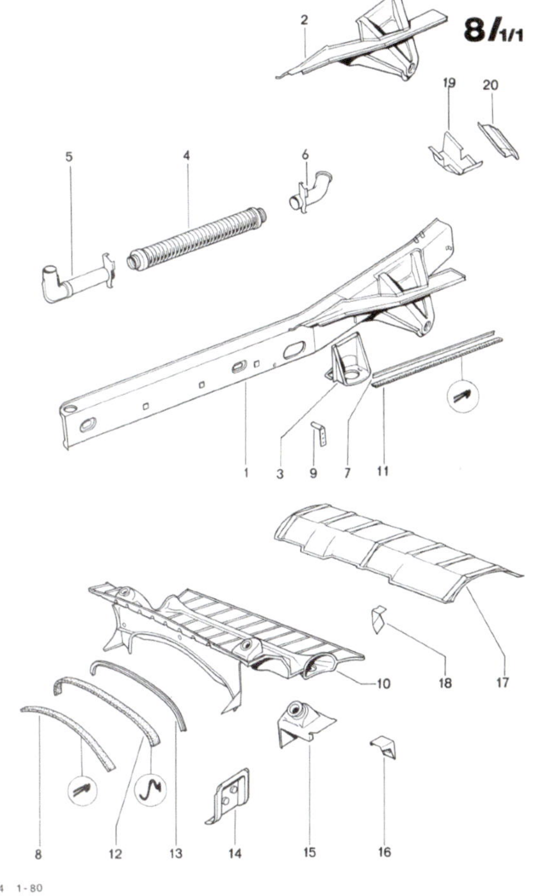

Illustration 8/1/1

1970-1971 upper firewall

panel was the brace and tube which made up the jack receiver (numbers 25 and 26). These receivers were accessed through a small rectangular hole in the outer rocker panel.

The longitudinal member made up the inner part of the threshold. It traversed the driver's compartment starting at the front of the door, curving upward and ending at the back of the engine bay. Sound deadening insulation covered the front half on 914-6 models, but four-cylinder cars had none. The rear part of the longitudinal had the pick-up for the control arm of the rear suspension. The 914-6 version was nearly identical to the four, lacking only the engine carrier brackets (*Illustration 8/1/1, number 3*). On the left side there were only two types, one for the four-cylinder cars and one for the sixes. On the right, things were more complicated. Modifications to improve the strength of the panel with internal reinforcement occurred on the 914-6 between 1970 and 1971, while the 914-4 was modified in 1972 and again in 1975, the latter possibly due to the relocation of the fuel pump and filter.

The rear wall of the passenger's compartment was also the firewall for the engine bay. The lower part (*Illustration 8/2, number 12*) was different on the 914-6, since the engine mount was located there. A change occurred at the 1972 model year, when the passenger's seat became movable and retractable seat belts were added. A subsequent modification was made in 1973, when the shift linkage was changed.

914-6 oil filler and oil line go through the engine compartment wall to hook up with oil tank inside the left rear fender

1972 and later upper firewall. Note depressed areas at upper corners for seatbelts

Engine Compartment and Rear Chassis

The inner rear quarter panel made up the side wall of the engine and rear luggage compartments. It was also the inner surface of the roll bar posts. Due to the location of the oil tank in the 914-6 (between the left rear inner and outer fenders), the four and six-cylinder cars did not share common left inner quarters. They did, however, use the same right-side panels.

The 914-6 GT and 916 differed from standard 914s by having strengthening plates welded to the outside of the inner fender around the rear suspension mounts. These plates were available through the dealer network, as well as reproductions from aftermarket sources, and are found on a variety of non-GTs.

In December 1972 (1973 model year) at chassis number 473 291 0937 US cars received an alteration described as a protection rail (*see photos next page*). There was also a triangular reinforcement at the base of the roll bar which added rigidity. These modifications coincided with the addition of steel beams in the doors mandated by US side-impact regulations. No further modifications were made.

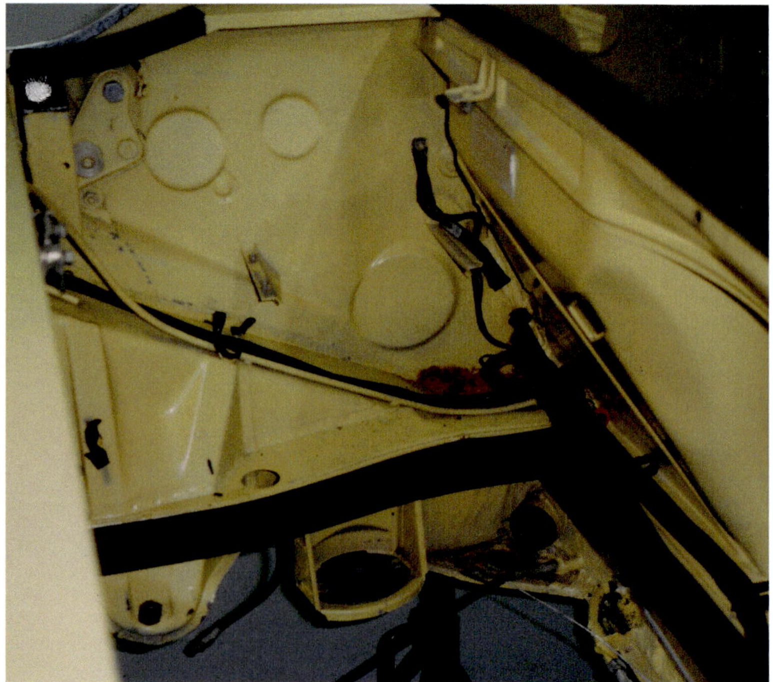
On four cylinder cars there were impressions where the 914-6 had holes for oil filler, oil line and oil filter (lower right)

Strengthening plates were fitted on 914-6 GT and 916 models

Two components that mount directly to the inner fender are perhaps best known for their failure rate. On each side a small bracket (*illustration 8/2, number 17*) was attached by spot welds to the inner quarter panel. The bracket served as the mounting point for the rear lid hinge pivot. Due to stress, often caused by non-lubricated pivot bolts, the brackets tended to *un-weld* themselves from the chassis. The first clue that something had gone awry was an elevation of one of the rear lid's forward corners.

914-6 engine compartment wall without protection rail. Note hinge bracket

The protetion rail above was added from December 1972

Battery tray included a hold down bracket for the ridge on the original battery

Battery tray and support were frequently damaged by battery acid

The second troublesome member in the engine compartment was the battery tray and support. This two-piece combination (*illustration 8/2, numbers 22 and 23*) was spot-welded in place on the passenger side inner quarter panel. This position, in part, offset the driver's weight. While good in theory, this location was perhaps not the best in practice. Exposure to the elements via the open grille above plus vibration and heat from the engine tended to take their toll. Battery acid would be at least partly at fault in weakening the support. Frequently, failure of the voltage regulator caused the battery to over-charge and *boil* through the caps. Rain water entering through the rear grille was also a cause of acid being washed down to the tray and support.

The weakened support would allow the battery to fall, though they generally did not fall too far, since the battery cables held them in place. Often they spilled some of the contents from their cells, which at best poured on to the chassis sheet metal or in the worst case emptied on to the fuel injection lines and right rear suspension mounting area. Originally, 914s had a small waffle-grained ABS plastic cap that partially covered the battery. A recall in July 1977 called the HO campaign, issued a large, flat, smooth plastic cover which covered the entire top of the battery.

The firewall between the engine compartment and interior beginning in the 1973 model year was covered with a thick tar-impregnated

The small original type battery cover. Note lack of insulating pad

Firewall insullation pad was added for the 1973 model year. Note also the HO campaign flat battery cover fitted to this 1976 2.0

rubber pad clipped and glued in place. On the interior side was a tar pad. These provided insulation from engine noise.

Mounted to the outer surface of the inner quarter panel in the roll bar area was a strengthening panel (*illustration 8/2, number 14*). This, as with the previous failure-prone components, was not modified during production.

Twin rubber flaps were added at the front of the engine compartment at the 1973 model year to aid cooling

The rear wall of the engine compartment and the floor of the rear luggage compartment was a multi-piece corrugated panel that covered the gearbox and exhaust system (*illustration 8/1/1, number 10*). It also incorporated the top mounts of the rear spring/shock absorber units, rear sway bar mounting brackets (optional equipment 1972 914-6 and 1973 and later four-cylinder cars) and the rear transmission mounting brackets. On the 914-6, the muffler shield was bolted to the floor panel, while the version for the four-cylinder cars was welded in place.

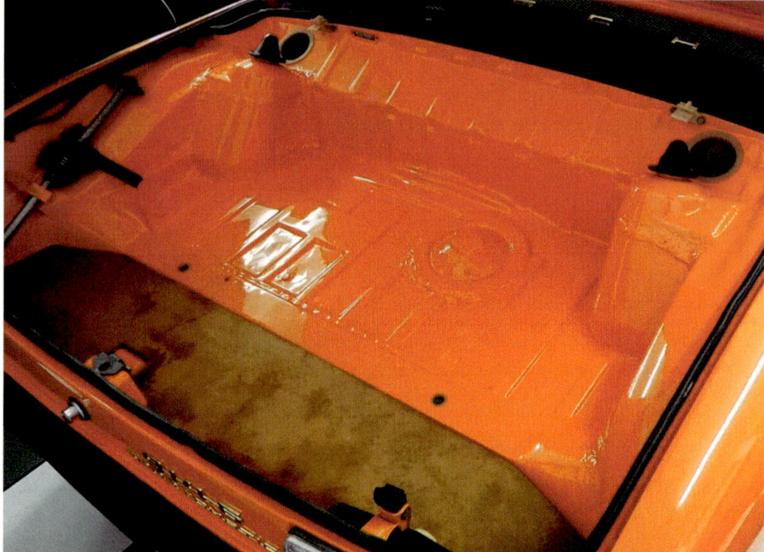
Rear compartment area with domed plug for Sportomatic transmission

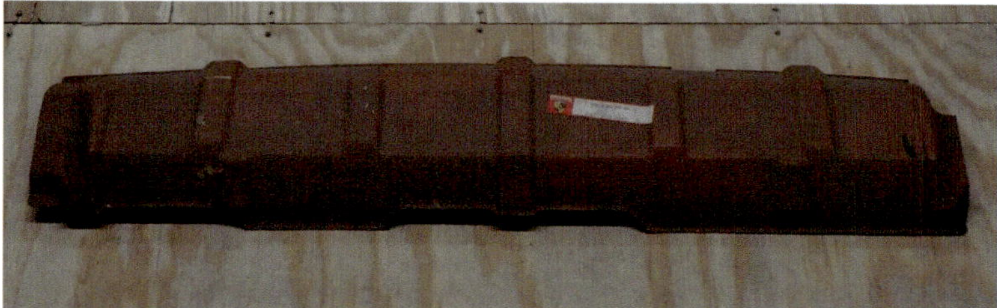
Muffler shield was welded on 4-cylinder cars and bolted on the 914-6

These two domed Phillips head bolts help secure the muffler shield on this unrestored 1970 914-6

Body

Front Bumper Area

The front bumper area of the first 914 models consisted of a lower front valance, bumper assembly and black polyurethane cap. The 1975 and 1976 models, due to the revised crash bumpers did not have the cap.

The valance was steel, finished with textured semi-gloss black paint. It wrapped under the nose and had a smooth curved design with two bulges along the bottom edge in front of where the transverse links from the front suspension were attached. This valance was used on all standard models. 914-6s fitted with the M471 option package introduced in March 1971, which included flared fenders and 6" Fuchs wheels, had a steel front valance hand-flared at the ends to blend with the widened fenders. Early versions may have been fiberglass.

In 1974 an optional front spoiler was offered on the Limited Edition model. It was made from white gel-coated, molded fiberglass (smooth finish on both sides) and featured a break in the middle somewhat reminiscent of the 1972 911S spoiler. Access to the towing hook was, at least in part, the reason for this break. Spoiler color varied on these Limited Edition cars, matching the color of the bumpers, rocker panels, rear valance, wheel centers and on US cars, negative side stripes. Colors were yellow on black cars or orange on white cars. This spoiler, in black only, was available as an option on other models through the 1976 model year.

Above the bumper was a foam-core polyurethane cap, black in color, with a textured surface. While it could take minor impacts without incident, unrepairable deformities from greater impacts, and cracks caused by ultraviolet light and/or internal rust formation as the cars

Stock front valance

Polyurethane bumper cap showing UV and minor internal rust damage

Flared steel valance on the M471 optioned 914-6

Orange painted Limited Edition front spoiler

The 1972 or earlier painted bumper

aged, frequently led to replacement of this part and the corresponding rear cap. This part was not necessary on the 1975 and 1976 models, which were fitted with the revised bumpers made necessary by US crash regulations.

The 1970 through 1974 bumper was a gently curved panel between valance and cap. Through 1972 there were two varieties. Standard bumpers were painted to match the car's exterior paint color. Chrome-plated bumpers were offered as part of the appearance group option package. These were also standard equipment on the 914-6. Bumpers on 914-6 GTs looked identical to the standard cap and bumper, but were a single part made of fiberglass. An opening for the front-mounted oil cooler was centrally placed on the lower edge.

The bumper/cap and valance on the 914-6 GT were made from fiberglass

1974 model with black bumper and optional spoiler

Optional appearance group chrome-plated bumper

For 1973 and 1974 models the color-keyed, painted bumpers were no longer offered; satin black versions were standard equipment. Their appearance blended better with the valance and cap panels. Those cars so fitted looked slightly less austere than the earlier models with painted bumpers. Chrome-plated bumpers were offered in the US, again in 1973, as part of the appearance group and in 1974 as optional equipment. Both types of US bumpers differed from earlier versions due to the holes for mounting small rubber guards and reinforcements on the inside of the face bar necessitated by crash standards. The guards, described on pages 42 and 51, were only on the front bumper in 1973, then front and rear for 1974.

The rest of the world had a slightly different scenario in 1973-1974. The 1970 through 1972 bumpers continued to be used, either in satin black or chrome finish, since no guards were fitted. The Swedish specification 914 of 1974 was fitted with a front bumper cap all its

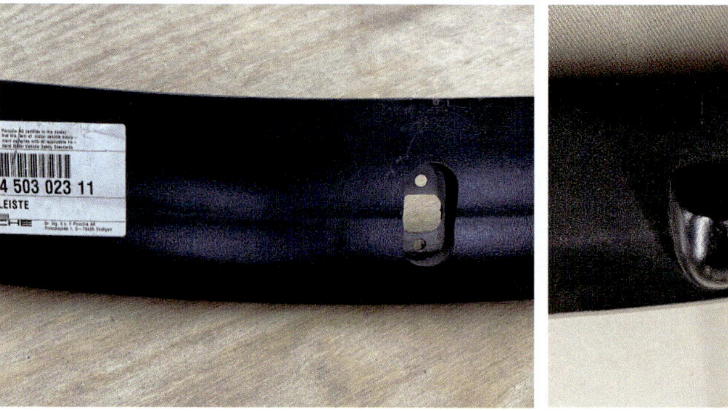

1974 Swedish spec. headlight washers were mounted on the bumper cap

1974 Limited Edition bumpers were either yellow or orange

1975-1976 front bumper

own with headlight washers incorporated. Again, both matte black and chrome varieties were offered. The washer nozzles were located on the bumper cap.

The bumper on 1975-1976 914s was considerably different, thanks again to US requirements. The new bumper received rave reviews for enhancing the appearance of the 914, when most manufacturers were plagued with protruding and ungainly bumpers. On the 914 the projecting black bumpers with accordion pleats made the front and rear of the car less blunt looking.

The black, synthetic rubber covered a steel bumper which on US and Canadian cars was mounted to self-restoring shock absorbers. A second version without shock absorbers was made for most of the rest of the world (Sweden again had headlight washers included). An extra

Standard US spec. front fender

Clip installed on 1975-1976 cars to secure the end of the bumper cover

916 front bumper with opening for oil cooler

channel was added to the side of the nose area which served as a support for the rear edge of the cover (*see photo below*).

An interesting variation on the theme was offered for the very limited production 916. The 916 bumper replaced all three front end components (bumper, cap and valance) and had driving or fog lights in the same location as 914s. It also had an opening for the front-mounted oil cooler. Again, a split-style spoiler was utilized. The 916's memory has been kept alive by numerous aftermarket companies that produce the front and rear look-alike bumpers, molded in fiberglass as were the originals. Had the 916 been put into production, based on impending impact regulations, the Porsche factory could have made the bumper from polyurethane and included proper reinforcement. The mounting hardware on one of the real 916s was visible in the form of two fasteners located to the outside of the driving lights.

Front Fenders

The steel front fenders on the 914 were identical from 1970 through 1974. A bracket was added for 1975 and 1976 models to hold the edge of the bumper covering in place. Two different versions were produced. The first, used in Italy, Denmark, Japan and the US had a provision for a turn indicator or side reflector. The rest of the world did not have these, so there were no holes in the fenders. Fenders were welded at the rear to the inner fender and at the front were welded to the inner nose panel, to lend structural rigidity to the chassis.

European spec. 914-6 without side light/reflector

Flared front fender, Euro spec. 914-6 with M471 option package

A separate steel fender flare was added for the 914-6 GT. The rectangular lines of this flare adapted well to the 914's squarish design. These flares were also fitted to the 916 and offered from mid-1971 on 914-6s equipped with the M471 option package.

Headlight Area and Hood

The 914 headlights were the first on a Porsche production car to be hidden from view. Steel panels, painted the color of the car, covered the retractable light unit. A small "blind" was positioned in front. This blind was held in place by three rubber plugs (with outward pointing tips) which allowed it to move harmlessly out of the way if something was caught between the light unit and blind as the headlight moved. Headlight covers and blinds were not interchangeable, left to right. No alterations were made from 1970 through 1976, and all markets shared the same parts.

Headlight cover and small blind were unchanged throughout production

Foam hood seal follows the shape of the hood around the headlight units

Front fender US spec. 916

The hood was also a universal component for all 914s. The featureless, slightly curved, outer steel skin covered a pressed steel substructure. Only the first few prototype 914-6s included the 911-style Porsche crest, although many owners subsequently fitted them. To re-

Steel hood used on all production 914s

Inside structure of the steel front hood

This gap in the front lid's substructure was included to accomodate an exterior fuel filler not incorporated in production 914s due to cost

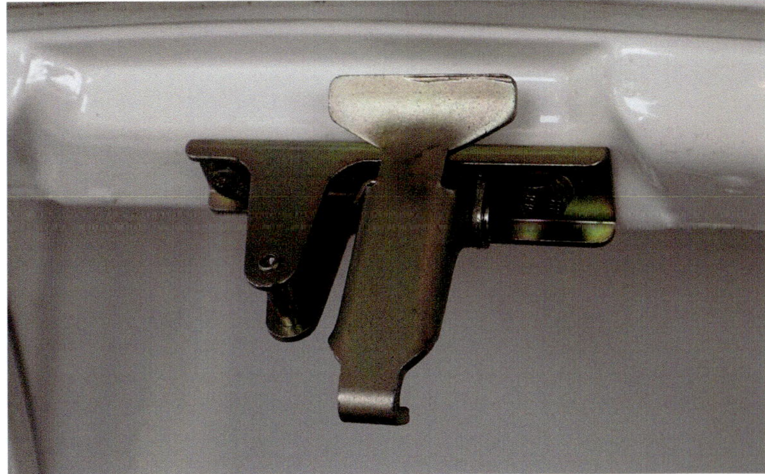
Front hood upper latch

duce weight, the hood on 914-6 GT cars was fiberglass. It was stiffened by strips of balsa wood bonded to the inner surface. The inner framework was also modified with cut-outs for shock tower clearance and rounding of the corners where the quick release hood pins penetrated.

The foam seal around the lid was identical in cross section to the one used on the 911. A second seal was on the partition separating the fuel tank from the luggage area. The upper latch attached to the hood via two bolts and featured a safety latch to prevent inadvertent opening if the lid was released at speed. Under normal circumstances the front hood was opened by a cable release mechanism operated from the driver's compartment. In the event of cable failure, there was an emergency access hole in the inner nose panel which allowed the hood to be opened once the bumper was removed. The hood was secured to the hinges by unpainted 13 mm headed bolts.

When unlatched, the hood was held open by a coil spring on each hinge. This reliable, inexpensive and uncomplicated system was superior to the costly, failure-prone pneumatic struts of the 911. The spring tension could be adjusted by the placement of the front mounting point.

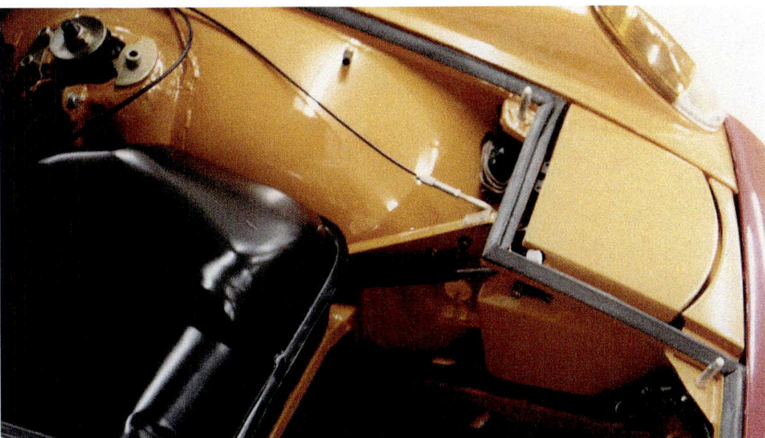
Corner plates installed on the 914-6 GT for hood pins

Inside the fibergalss 914-6 GT were stengthening braces made of balsa wood

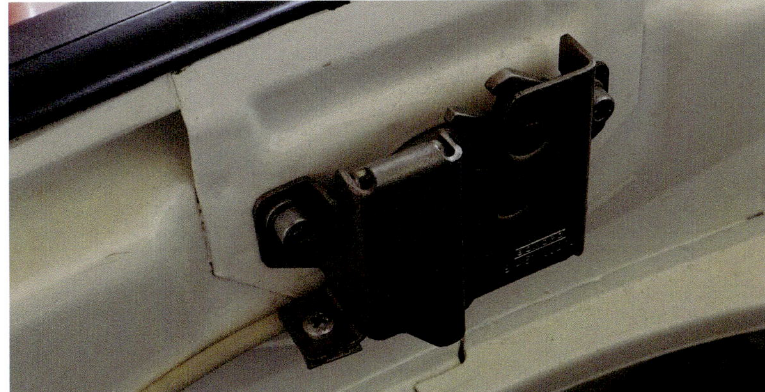
Front hood lower latch

Adjustable hood spring

Cowl housed windshield wipers and washers

Cowl Area, Windshield

This area included the front windshield frame and small cowl panel directly behind the hood. On this panel, the windshield wipers and washer jets were mounted. In its center was the fresh air inlet for the driver's compartment. The gaps between front fenders and cowl were bridged by a pair of black vinyl seals. In very early prototype cars these seals were omitted.

The windshields of all Canadian, Swedish and US market 914s were laminated glass and were offered clear (standard) or tinted (extra cost option). The latter version was tinted uniformly throughout and did not have a darker sun screen band at the top. Buyers in other countries had the same choice on the 914-6 and 1973-1976 914 2.0s, but the lesser models came with non-tinted, tempered glass standard. The two laminated windshields described above were optional. On 916s the windshield contained the radio antenna. Regardless of glass type, the windshield was held in place by a 6 mm butyl seal and positioned by two rubber spacers. The anodized trim was attached by 19 plastic clips.

Windshied area 1970-1976

The 916 featured a radio antenna imbedded in the windshield

Early metal finished cowl to fender seam

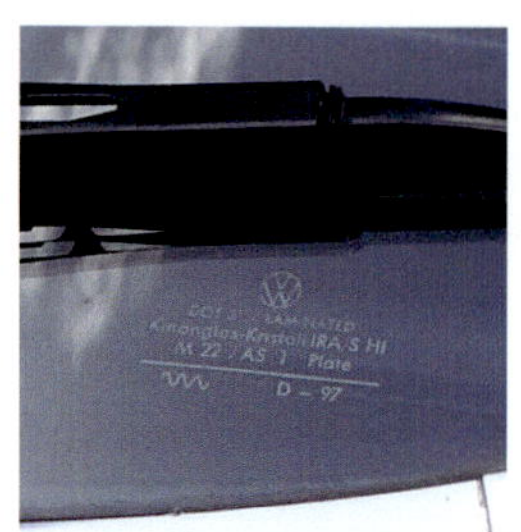

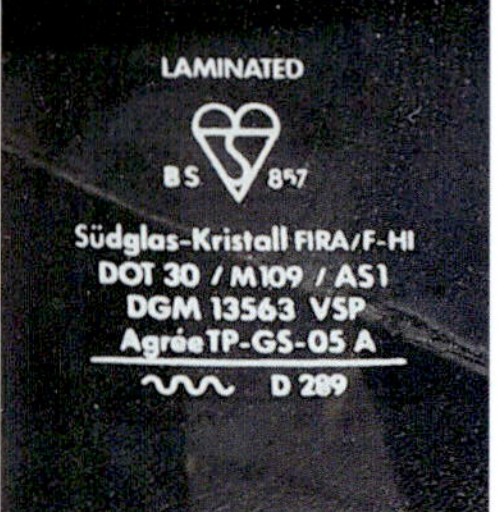

Windshield "bugs" 1970 US, 1974 Japan, 1976 US

Top, Headliner

One feature that set the 914 apart from its contemporaries was the lightweight removable top. Made from molded, fiberglass-reinforced plastic with internal bracing, the top was coated with a textured matte black finish.

A major change in the top was made during July 1973 at chassis number 473 292 6222. Alterations were made to the top, headliner,

Early style top

Early (left) and late (right) front top detail

front mounting area and rear seal to reduce squeaking and increase sealing.

The front top mount consisted of two toggle-type latches on the top, while the rear latch mechanisms were on the roll bar. These rear latches had black steel bases from 1970 through 1974 and black plastic bases in 1975 and 1976. The side and rear weather strips were mounted on the top with the front seal on the windshield frame. Side seals were changed only once, between the 1973 and 1974 model years, when an extra lip was added for better sealing. The rear seal change was mentioned above. Both rear seal and side seals involved only minor revisions, and the later seals can be used on early cars.

The 916 differed from standard production cars by having a steel top, welded to the windshield frame in the front and to the roll bar in the rear. A variety of headliner materials, including leather, perforated vinyl and carpet replaced the gray felt version found in the standard 914. The earliest 650 or so 914s and 914-6s and all 1970 and 1971 914s without the optional appearance group had no headliner.

Front top latch

Rear "silent bloc" rear top latch

Rear latch, early

Rear latch, late

Early (left) and late (right) side window seal profiles

Steel top found only on the 916

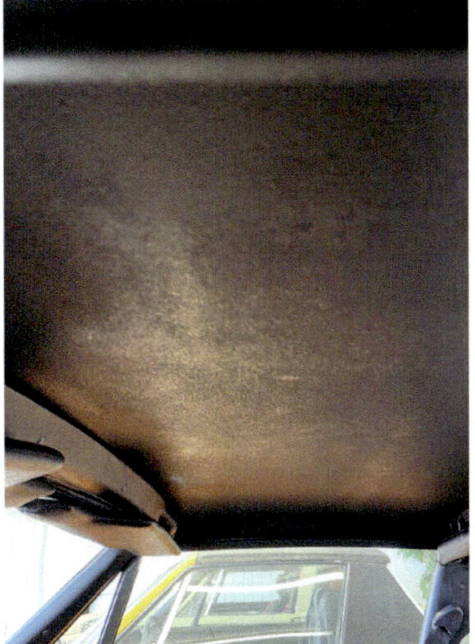

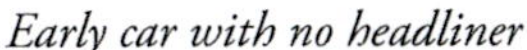

Early car with no headliner

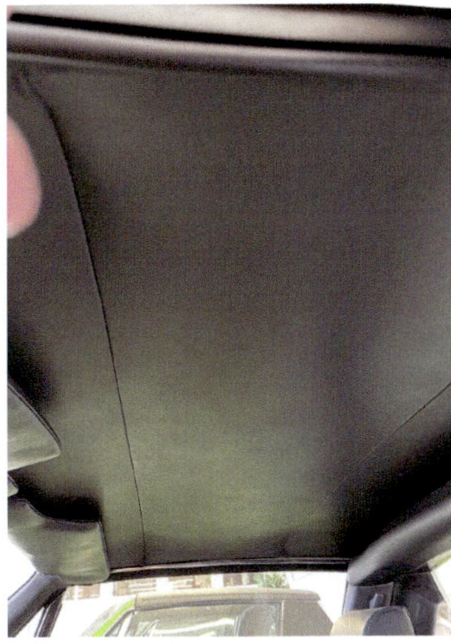

Leather headliner, 916

Felt headliner, 1970

The GT top was braced in different ways to add structural rigidity

The 914-6 GT was by definition a closed car. If the top was removed it could not be classified as a true GT, and thus would not have been eligible to compete in the FIA under 2-litre GT class. Rather than having a steel top fashioned in similar fashion to the 916, steel braces were bonded to the inner surface of the fiberglass top on some cars and additional strengthening bars added in others.

Doors, Rocker Panels

The outer appearance of the door remained unchanged throughout the production run of the 914. The inner structure was modified around 1000 cars into the 1973 model year, due to the change in the window channels and lift mechanism (*see page 48*). A subsequent change came later in 1973 when a strengthening bar was added.

US-bound cars saw the incorporation of steel side guards, as dictated by new DOT safety standards. These weighty additions were not found on non-US specification cars. The latch mechanism on the door had been changed at the end of the 1971 model year.

Upside down doors, early (top) and late (bottom)

Elements of the strengthening beam visible at the front of this cutaway door

Standard steel rocker panel

Painted rocker panel, 1974 Limited Edition

Flared fiberglass 916 rocker panels

The outer rocker panel covers were a steel stamping mounted by bolts fore and aft with plastic rivets in between. They were painted matte black with the exception of the Limited Edition models, where they matched the front and rear valances. A black plastic plug capped the jack sockets.

The 914-6 with M471 option package, 914-6 GT and 916 models shared rocker panels that were flared at each end to match the fender extensions. These were the only fiberglass 914 rocker panels installed at the factory, although many owners of 914s frequently replaced rusted originals with fiberglass reproductions. The original factory GT versions had the factory part number in raised letters on the top of the panel. ABS rocker panel covers with raised Porsche lettering were a dealer installed item in the US.

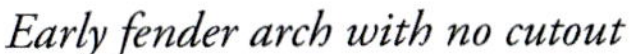

Early fender arch with no cutout

Late fender arch with cutout

Rear Quarter Panels

The rear quarter panel of the 914 was modified after the end of the 1970 model year. The inner lip of the rear arch was modified in 1971 to provide greater tire clearance (*see photos above*). As with the front fender, a small tab was added in 1975 to hold the bumper covering flush to the body. The quarter panel incorporated the lock post and side roll bar panel in an assembled pressing. The small lip around the rear wheel arch was quite a contrast to the large rectangular steel flares fitted to the 916 and 914-6 GT models which extended the width of each fender by approximately two inches.

Standard rear fender

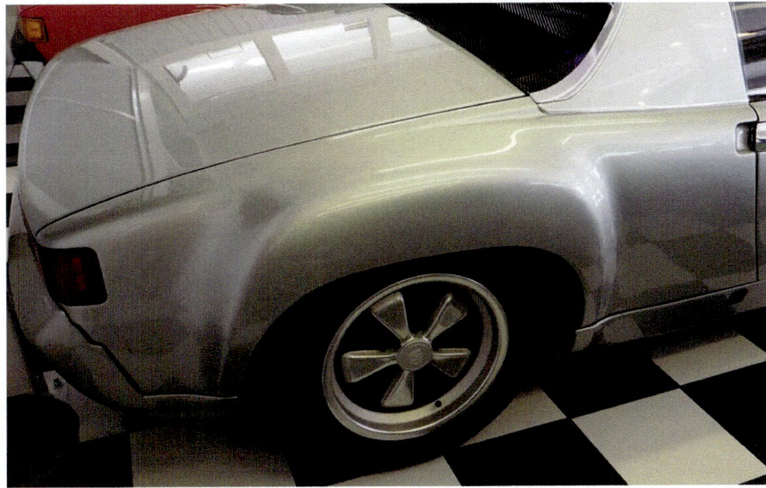

916 fender with steel flare

Roll bar top with appearance group

Joining the two quarter panels across the roll bar top was a nearly flat panel painted body color on cars without vinyl-covered roof pillars. On cars with upholstered pillars, the top panel was vinyl covered.

Lock Posts

The lock post had a fresh air exhaust vent with a black plastic exterior and a felt washer behind from 1972 through 1976, with earlier cars having empty holes. Also located in the lock post was the striker plate for the door latch. There were three different versions. The first type was used until late in the 1971 model year. The second version was used from that point through mid-1973. These differed from the first type by having a metal stop tab incorporated which prevented the door closing too far. The final variety with slightly altered tab, which kept the door from rattling and added structural integrity was used from mid-1973 through 1976.

Engine Compartment Lid

Over the engine compartment was a lid with a latch operated via cable release from the driver's compartment. This lid had a painted panel at the front and a black mesh grille at the rear. The hinges were

Early striker plate (left), middle one with small straight stop tab, and late style with larger stop tab. Note also no plastic exhaust vent on the early car on left

Engine lid, 914-6

at the sides, close to the rear window. Flanking this lid were two small panels that matched the theme of the lid.

The 914-6 differed from the four-cylinder variety by having no provision for attaching the drain tray (*described on page 49*). There was a modification in 1973 to provide a bolting surface for the improved drain tray. The 916 and 914-6 GT had a slightly different engine lid with a larger grille area for improved cooling. Both types used the same simple hinges and torsion bar springing device (weaker tension for the lighter six lid) to keep it open. The release mechanism on the

Torsion bar system on the 914-6 had weaker tension due to lack of drain tray

Four-cylinder drain tray kept water off of the engine. Note also upper latch bolt

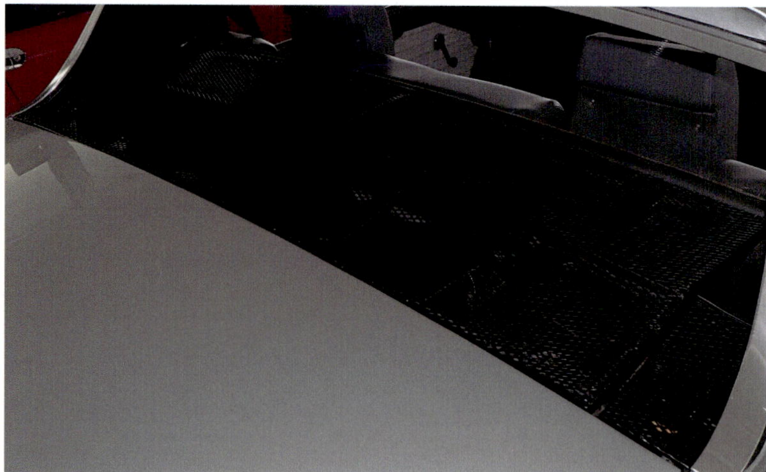

Engine lid, 916

Engine lid release pull located on the driver's side firewall

Cable-operated engine lid latch mechanism

GT had a Volkswagen plastic release handle and protruded from the panel to the left of the lid.

On the lid was a simple 90-degree bent bolt that locked into the cable-released lower latch on the body. The front of the engine lid was attached to the back wall by two hinge brackets via 6 mm bolts. The hinges were slotted for adjustment. The hinge bracket to which the hinge bolted fatigued with time when the lid was raised beyond the normal angle. When these brackets eventually broke the lid could not be opened. Replacements were never provided by Porsche, but are currently available on the aftermarket.

Trunk Lid

The rear trunk lid was bolted to the rear hinges with four 13 mm head bolts painted body color. It used a somewhat complicated hinging device and the same type springing medium as the engine lid. This was prone to failure, generally due to rust formation between the pivoting shoulder bolt and the hinge. Frequent lubrication could have prevented this, but no one predicted the problem.

The nylon torsion bar roller was modified at the 1974 model year. The later version was wider and about half the diameter. The earlier style had a tendency to break; many pre-1974 cars have been updated, since the parts are interchangeable.

The change in the roller was the only modification to the rear lid area. The latch mounted to the rear of the lid was a simple pin and spring device. Two Volkswagen rubber bump stops, also seen on 911 front and rear lids were found on the rear of the lid.

Euro spec. 914-6 tail panel/rear lid area. Note lack of letters on engine lid

Rear lid inner structure. Note also upper lid latch and plated hinge bolts

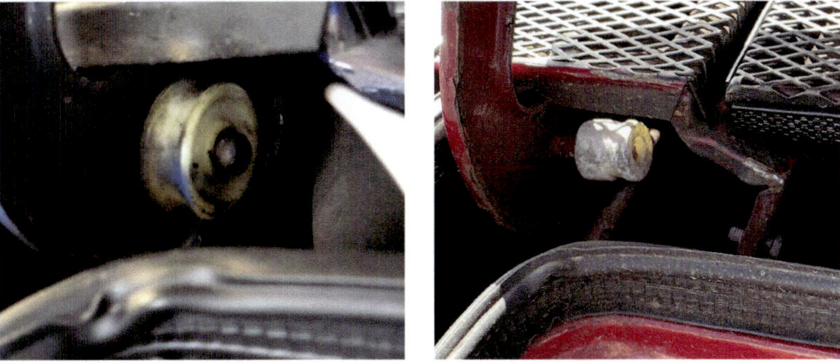

Both early roller (left) and late roller (right) were made of nylon

The 914-6 GT was fitted with a fiberglass rear lid with balsa wood stiffeners. Its construction was similar to the front lid (*described on page 31*).

GT rear lid with balsa wood stiffening

Tail Panel

The rearmost body panel was similar to the inner nose panel in that it served as the mount for the bumper. Unlike the nose, however, a portion of the panel was visible above the bumper as the exterior of the car. It housed the taillights, rear lid release and model designation scripts.

Cars built in 1969 had a slightly different inner structure than the one used from 1970 through 1974. When crash bumpers were added in 1975, the tail panel was again modified, and a US spec. version was produced, as well as one for the rest of the world. The difference was the impact resistant shock absorber mounts on the US cars.

1970 914-6

Subtle changes were evident by 1974

Additional reinforcements for the rear bumpers were added for US cars in 1975. Note also lower latch for rear lid

Location of shock absorbers for the US impact absorbing bumpers used in 1975 and 1976

Rear Bumper and Valance

Rear bumpers followed the same progression as the front bumper. For 1970 through 1972 there were chrome and painted varieties. The chrome version used in 1970 had a slightly larger plate area and can be differentiated from later versions by its sharper, angular bends around the plate recess. In 1973 and 1974, the painted ones were replaced by matte black, and chrome remained optional. US specification cars for 1974 differed from the rest of the world by having holes for rubber bumper guards and bumper reinforcements. All of these bumpers had a recessed area in the center where the license plate was mounted.

Through 1974 a black polyurethane cap piece was positioned above the bumper in the same manner as up front and suffered from the same ailments mentioned on page 27, but even more so, due to the narrower recessed section where the license plate was mounted. In the lower lip toward the middle were two license plate lights. The 914-6 GT had a rear bumper identical in appearance to standard bumper and cap, but was made in a single piece from fiberglass. Additional bracing behind the bumper guards was added in 1974.

The bumper used in 1975 and 1976 was much like the corresponding front bumper: black synthetic rubber which covered a steel bumper. US and Canadian bumpers were mounted on self-restoring

Early painted rear bumper and four-cylinder valance

Early chrome-plated rear bumper and six-cylinder valance

Black rear bumper used in 1973-1974 for 914s without appearance group

1974 US spec. chrome-plated late-style rear bumper and late (short) valance

1975-1976 US spec. rear bumper

1974 Limited Edition painted rear bumper and late-style rear valance

Some M471 914-6 models had no rear valance

The fiberglass 916 rear bumper

shock absorbers, while those for the rest of the world had fixed mounts. As on the front bumper, accordion pleats were molded into the textured surface. The license plate and plate lights (shared with period 911s) were found in the central recessed area.

The rear valance mounted below the bumper and gently curved under, covering the exhaust system. For 1970 and 1971, the tail pipe extended through a round hole on the left (driver's) side of the valance. The four-cylinder car had this hole several inches inboard of the 914-6 opening. The M471 optioned 914-6 and GT had no rear valance.

In January 1972 the valance was shortened so that it could no longer accumulate road debris and snow. This provided the associated benefits of improved appearance and engine cooling. They were easily differentiated from the earlier versions, since the tail pipe was set into a recess in the lower part of the valance rather than being surrounded by it. The opening was also shifted several inches away from the car's center (same location as on the earlier 914-6). These steel valances were painted to match the rocker panels and front valances. No further changes were made through 1976.

The final bumper type was used on the 916. It was a one-piece molded fiberglass unit that replaced the bumper cap, bumper and lower valance. The license lights and plate were again in the central recessed area. The exhaust exited at the lower left.

Exterior Trim

Front Bumper

The bumpers of the 914 were relatively free of ornamentation. Trim consisted of guards, grilles and driving or fog lights.

From 1970 through 1974 grilles were present in the front bumper. The Hella horns were visible through the grilles. Actually, only one horn was supplied as standard equipment, the second being part of the optional appearance group. A Hella 335 Hz horn was standard and mounted on the left side, while the optional Hella 400 Hz was on the right.

1975-1976 cars had smaller Hella VW-sourced horns located behind the lower valance toward the front of the trunk floor. Again, the right side horn was optional.

Four types of grilles were supplied, depending on the bumper finish and whether driving/fog lights were fitted. Cars built in 1969 as early 1970 model cars had metal grilles, while all later grilles were plastic. These were painted to match the bumper finish, or when chrome bumpers were fitted, they were vacuum-metal chrome-plated. Left and right grilles were not interchangeable. Grilles on black bumpers (1973/1974) always had chrome finish. The grilles on Limited

Horn location for 1970-1974 914s

Early 914-4 without appearance group had no right side horn

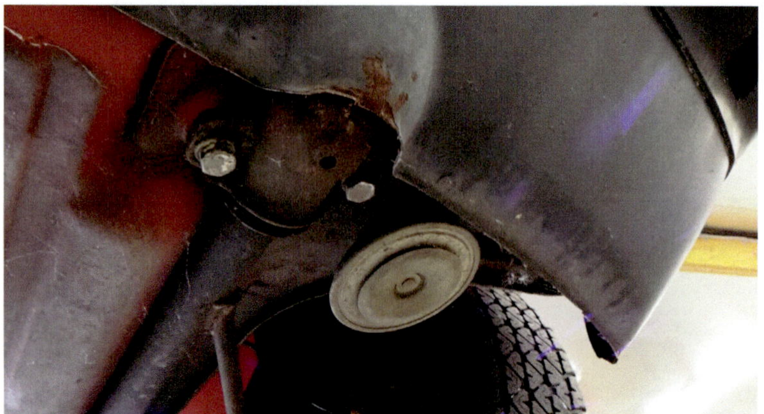

Revised horn locaion 1975-1976

Early painted horn grilles

Chrome-plated grilles were used on 1973-1974 black bumpers

Black grilles with US spec. foglight 1974 Limited Edition — note horn on right

Edition cars were black.

Several different types of auxiliary lights were optional, depending on preferences and national regulations. A total of seven types were offered between 1970 and 1974 with four additional types available for 1975 and 1976.

The round lights used through the 1974 model year were manufactured by Hella. They came in the following varieties:

1. Driving light with H-3 bulb, white
2. Driving light with H-3 bulb, yellow (France)
3. Driving light with H-1 bulb, white (Italy)
4. Fog light with non-halogen bulb, white (US)
5. Fog light with H-3 bulb, white
6. Fog light with H-3 bulb, yellow (France)
7. Fog light with H-1 bulb, white (Italy)

Driving lights, not legal in the US, had less fluting of the lenses so the beam was narrower and longer than that of the fog light. The French specification light units had yellow lenses (not bulbs) but were otherwise identical to the standard unit. The lenses on the Italian specification light units were the same as the standard unit; however the reflector was altered for the different bulb type. The US fog light had both unique lenses and reflectors. All of these lights had black housings and silver rear mounting brackets.

Original Euro spec. H-3 driving light

Later production replacement H-3 driving light. Note lens differences

US bulb-type fog light

Painted grille with French spec. driving light. Corporate Archives Porsche AG

US spec. fog light

The lights used on 1975 and 1976 were rectangular and were manufactured by Bosch in four varieties:

1. Driving light, white
2. Driving light, yellow (France)
3. Fog light, white (US)
4. Fog light, yellow (not for US or Japan)

All of these lights used the same H-3 halogen bulbs, housings and reflectors; only the lenses were different. When not fitted with one of these lights, this era 914 did not have the holes cut in the bumper material.

Front bumper guards used 1973-1974 on US 914s and factory license bracket

Front bumper guards used on some 1975-1976 US spec. cars

1975-1976 cars without fog/driving lights had no cut outs in the bumper

Due to crash standards set by the US D.O.T., the first bumper guards appeared in 1973. They were large rectangular synthetic rubber blocks which were mounted with two studs and nuts and located just inside the grilles. They were used through the 1974 model year. There was a metal support behind the guards between the face bar and inner nose. Rear guards are described on page 51.

Most of the US received a front bumper without separate guards for 1975 and 1976, but California and Maryland had regulations which required that small guards be added to the impact absorbing bumpers on these cars. From observation, it appears that the small guards were included on US spec. cars sold in other areas, as well.

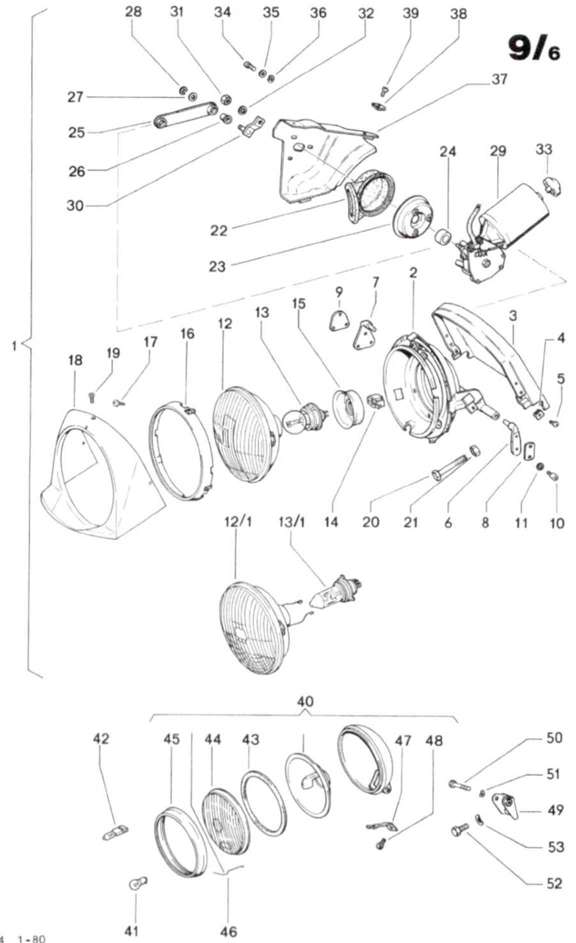

Illustration 9/6

Early headlight pivots had rounded tips

A final item of bumper trim was the headlight washer fitted to Swedish specification 914s starting in 1974. The 1974 version was located on the bumper cap; the later version was on top of the rubber bumper cover (*see photos page 28*).

Headlights

The hide-away headlight units of the 914 were fairly complicated. The rear pivots were bolted to the inside of the light box in such a way that when they were unbolted, the entire headlight unit lifted out from the top. The outer pivot mounted with two bolts and the inner had three (*numbers 6 and 7, illustration 9/6*). These were modified only once at the 1971 model year. The early style had rounded tips, while the late version was squared (see photo).

The headlight retainer (*number 2*) mounted via the pivots in the rear. A change in the retainer occurred in 1971 when the pivot changed. A short lever (*number 25*), steel from 1970 through 1974 and plastic thereafter, was attached to the inside surface connecting it with the motor (*number 29*) which made it move up and down. This lever passed through a brush-type device on 1970 through 1972 cars. This was deleted in 1973 when the lever was covered by a rubber boot.

The retainer was made from steel pressings and tubes welded together and finished in a matte gray zinc coating. The top of the retainer was covered by the headlight cover or cap (number 3), attached by sheet metal screws. Covering the retainer from below (or from the front when the lights were up) was a plastic headlight surround (number 18). This was white from 1970 through 1973 and black on later cars.

Early white plastic headlight surround and stainless steel retainer

Late black plastic headlight surround with black steel retainer

Behind the headlight box was the electric headlight motor. These came in left and right versions and had a black plastic circular knob on their rear surface which could be manually turned to raise or lower the light unit in case the motor failed. Motors were modified in 1973 and 1975. The changes consisted of different electrical connections. A black (or gray March through early May 1974) plastic cover (number 37) concealed the linkage between the motor and retainer.

Most 914s had black linkage covers. Headlight motor above

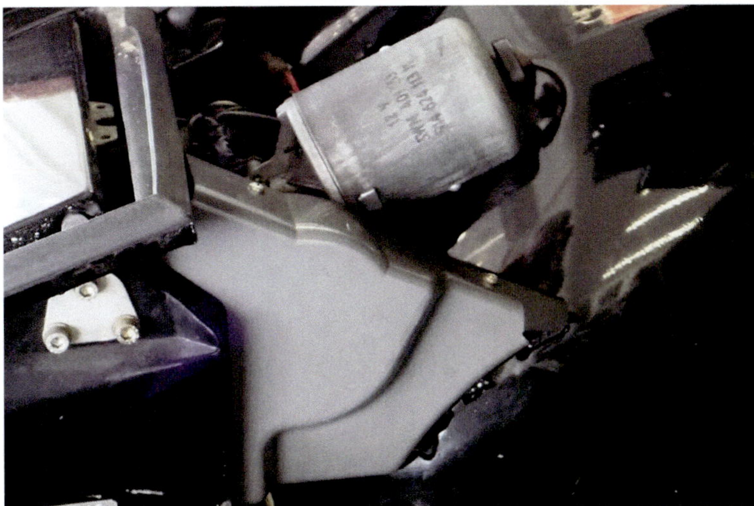

Gray linkage covers used March-May 1974 were found on most Limited Editions

The US turn signal unit had amber lens and one bulb, two bulbs everywhere else

The majority of other countries had the lens on the left, Italian 914s on the right

Headlights came in a number of varieties. The standard unit for most of the world was an asymmetrical type made by Hella with removable tungsten bulbs. French specification cars were fitted with yellow bulbs. Buyers in right hand drive countries received a light which projected an appropriate pattern. It is worth noting here that right-hand steering was not offered for any 914 model, although eleven conversions were done by Crayford in the UK.

US specification cars were fitted with sealed-beam light units. At chassis number 473 290 8292 in November 1972, during the 1973 model year, headlights were upgraded from 50/40 watt to 60/50 watt units. Brands used for sealed beam units likely varied, though later cars seem to frequently have GE headlights.

H-4 halogen light units were offered in 1973 as optional equipment, except in the US. Both Hella and Bosch versions were fitted for right-hand traffic cars, with Hella only for left. Yellow bulbs were again standard fare in France. In the US, halogen lights were still taboo and were not available during 914 production years.

The final headlight component was the ring which held the light to the retainer. These were stainless steel from 1970 through 1974. Later rings were black painted steel (*see photos page 43*).

GT headlights were operated by pneumatic struts, which eliminated the heavy electric motors. An interesting one-in/two-out splitter was located on the left inner wheel house for the cables that held the lights down.

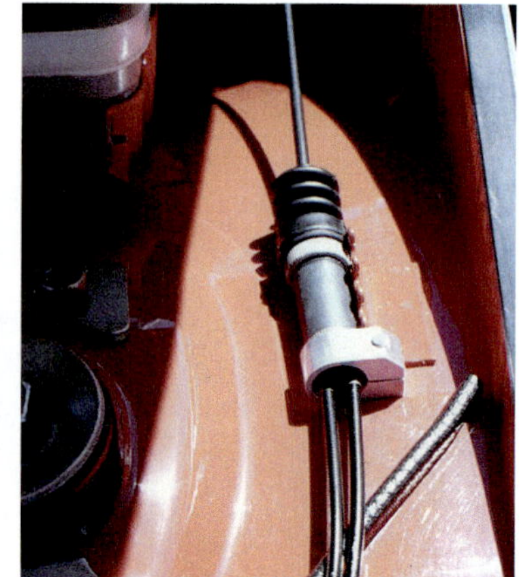

GT headlights operated much differently than production versions

Turn Signal and Side Marker

Front turn signal units came in three basic styles. The US-type had an amber lens and a single dual filament bulb which performed both running light and turn signal functions. Italian cars used the same housing but had a clear lens.

The rest of the world had a two-bulb signal unit which had a clear running light at the bottom and an amber turn signal at the top. A metal partition separated the two parts of the housing.

Moving rearward, the side marker light was located on the side of the front fender. These round lights were amber in color. On US specification cars these functioned as reflector and were illuminated when parking lights or headlights were on. Cars built for the Italian, Japa-

Side marker units: US, left and Japan, right

Subtly different side marker positioning when flares were fitted

Early cowl vent with no screen

A plastic screen was added to the cowl vent in June 1973

nese and Danish markets had a different lens, fluted similarly to the front signal lens. They acted as turn signals, not reflectors, on these cars. No modifications were made to these parts. On cars with flared fenders these lights were mounted lower and more forward (see photo). These lights were not found on cars sold in other countries.

Cowl Area

The cowl area was home for the windshield wipers and washer jets. The fresh air ventilation system drew its air through intake holes in the cowl between the wipers. Starting in June 1973, a plastic screen was installed below these holes to keep debris from entering. A new seal was incorporated at this time.

The wiper mechanism was not shared by four and six-cylinder cars. The different components consisted of arms, blades, motor and crank mechanism. The hardware securing the arms to the pivots was the same on all 914s, as well as contemporary 911s.

Wiper arms were finished in satin black. The left arm was slightly curved, while the right arm had an angled bend at the blade end. They parked on the left on all models. The 914-6 was equipped with the arms and blades used on the 1970 911s. There was a choice (Porsche's choice not the buyer's) of Bosch or SWF arms with blades to match. Four-cylinder cars had their own arms made by SWF and shared the blades with the six. 1971 and later 911s also used these arms.

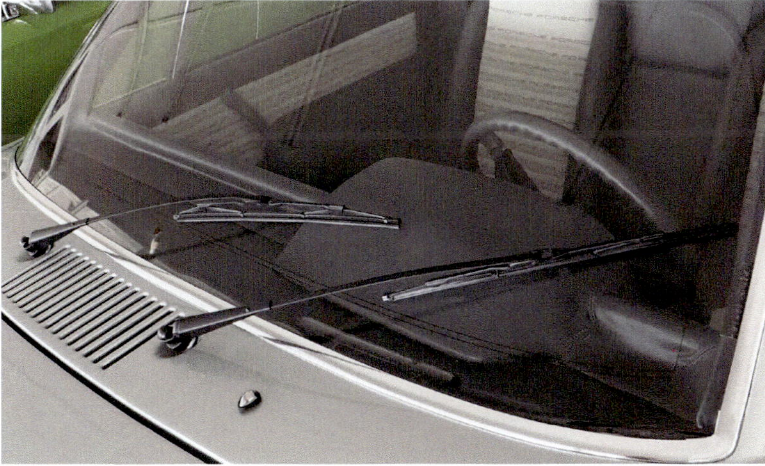

Wipers, 914-6

The 914-6 wiper motor had three speeds, like the 911, while the four had only two. The difference between the cranking mechanisms was necessary due to the way that the motors mounted to them.

The windshield washer jets were on the cowl to the outside of the wiper pivots. They were the same as those found on contemporary 911s, dual-nozzle, aluminum covered, rubber with removable check valves below. In or around June 1973 a revised one-piece black plastic washer jet without check valve was introduced and was used through the duration of production. The remainder of the washer system is described in the section on luggage compartment (*page 57*).

Windshield

Windshields came in several varieties, as described on page 32, but the trim was the same. Three anodized aluminum pieces surrounded

Windshield washer nozzles, early (left) and late (right)

Left side arm on the 914-4 had a slight bend and parked lower

Windshield chassis number plate 1974 (US)

the windshield, the left and right pieces each extending half way across the top. These and the lower piece were spliced together by connecting clips, two identical lower corner clips and an upper piece, which covered the ends of the trim. The trim was press-fit onto 19 plastic clips (*number 16, Illustration 8/8*).

In early 1973, all 914s with the appearance group option package featured front windshield frames upholstered with the same vinyl used on the rear roof pillars. Unlike the rear, there was no metal trim piece at the bottom edge. This was a short-lived feature confined to

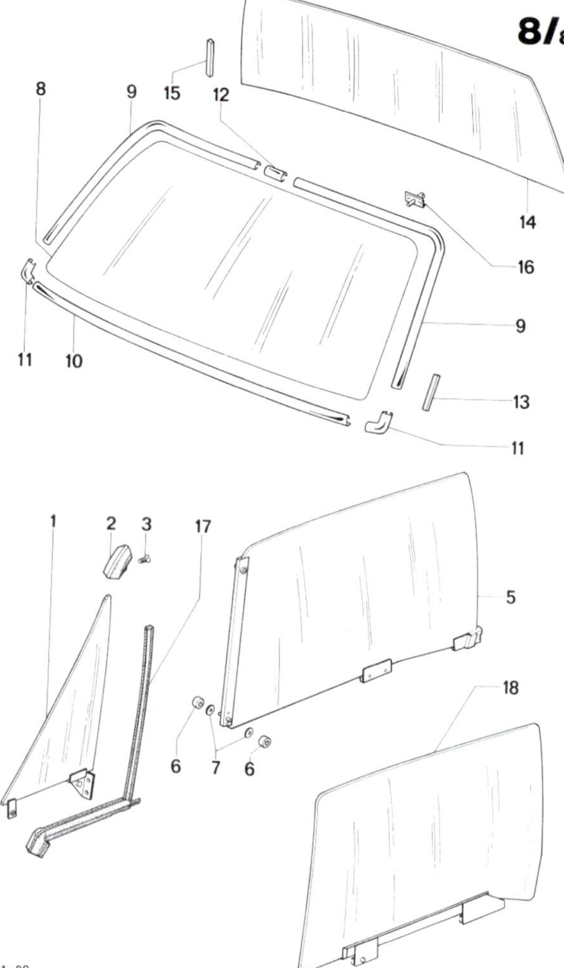

Illustration 8/8

Windshield chassis number plate 914-6 (US)

the first 1000 or so 1973s. Incorrect information in the parts manual indicates more extensive use, giving a part number for 1972 and earlier cars.

On US-spec. cars in the lower left corner, inside the glass, was a sheet metal plate stamped with the chassis number. It was riveted in place.

European 914-6 windshield trim. Note lack of chassis number plate

Rare early-1973 upholstered A-pillars

Early driver's side mirror

Door Trim

The doors were devoid of much ornamentation, but did feature side mirror, door handle and occasionally side stripes, in addition to the side window and trim.

The side mirror was rectangular and mounted on the driver's side door. It was modified for 1972 by altering the mirror size (late ones were wider and shorter) and the angle and cross-section of the arm (later ones were more round). Right-side mirrors were fitted in Sweden and an optional convex right-side mirror is listed, although it is uncertain when and where they were offered. The nut cages for mounting mirrors were present in all right doors, making it possible to fit them to cars not originally so equipped.

The 914 door handle

The 914's unusual door handles were flush-mounted and consisted of a front part which included the lock cylinder and a hinged rear part. They were made from chrome-plated pot metal which was failure-prone due to metal fatigue. The plastic slider also frequently broke during use.

Positive stripes were a common period accessory

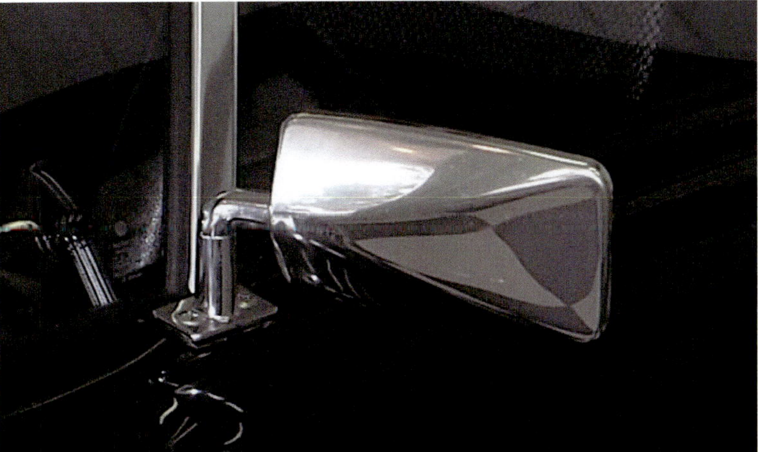

Late driver's side mirror

Early passenger's side mirror

Side stripes are not officially mentioned in the parts book; however, it is certain that they were available in 1970. These were the same positive stripes used on the 911 of that time. Positive means that the letters were the color of the stripe, which contrasted with the later negative stripe, where the letters were the color of the car. Positive stripes came in black or white and were printed on a clear mylar strip with adhesive on the back.

In 1974 the negative stripe replaced the earlier type. They were die-cut mylar with adhesive on the back. Colors offered included black, white, yellow, orange and green. These stripes were standard on all US Limited Edition models. Porsche stripes were likely only used on

Negative stripes came in yellow and orange on Limited Edition models

Early (left) and late (right) side window channels

US cars, since elsewhere the 914 was marketed through Volkswagen. Stripes were also fitted as dealer-installed options.

Side windows and frames were modified only once. The first style, used from 1970 through early 1973, used an unusual lightweight tubular regulator which incorporated front and rear glass channels that contained no weather strips. A metal strip was attached on the leading edge of the side window, and small plastic rollers (*number 6, illustration 8/8, see page 46*) aligned the glass in the frame. A plastic and metal guide was located at the rear bottom corner of the window.

From roughly one thousand cars into the 1973 model year a more conventional system was used. Front and rear channels now contained flocked rubber weather strips. The window no longer had metal on its leading edge. With the new window came a modification of the cap at the top of the rear channel.

The front triangular side glass, which did not open, stayed the same throughout 914 production. The plastic cap and the seal below and behind the glass were also never modified. Both side windows were available clear or optionally tinted. The side windows used on 914-6 GTs were generally the standard glass ones found on production cars.

Early (left) and late (right) side window channel rear caps

Roll Bar

Standard on four-cylinder 914s from 1970 through 1973 was a painted rear top support area. Metal trim, which covered the trailing edge of the side and top of this roll bar, was painted the color of the car in 1970-1972 and was black anodized in 1973 and on 1974 Limited Edition models.

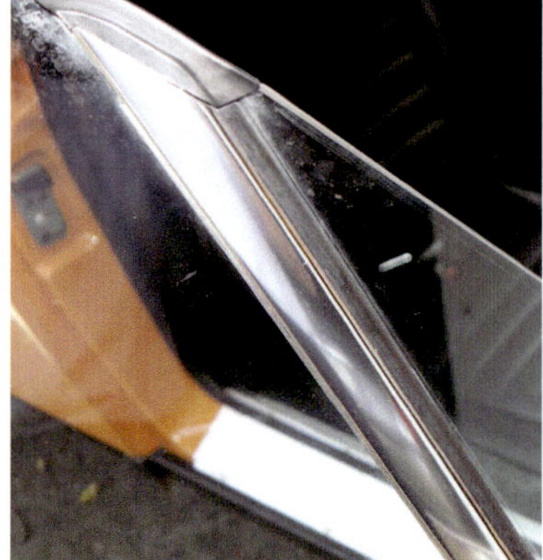

Plastic front side glass cap

The optional appearance group trim for the roll bar (standard on the 914-6), consisted of three vinyl panels which covered the roof pillars and top of the roll bar. The rear trim pieces (painted on the standard car) were bright anodized aluminum as were two additional pairs of trim pieces, one at the base of the pillar and one at the top. Vinyl trimmed roll bars were standard from 1974 through 1976. On 1973 cars without appearance group, the trim was black anodized.

The 916 had a non-removable steel top painted to match the body color. The roof pillars were also painted and used anodized trim like on appearance group cars.

The rear window was available in two types, plain and heated (optional). Unlike the other windows, tinted glass was not available.

Roll bar trim, 1970-1972 standard

Roll bar trim, appearance group

Roll bar trim, 1974 Limited Edition

Roll bar trim, 916

Optional rear window defogger

Engine Lid

The engine grille was semi-gloss black painted metal and fitted to the rear half of the engine lid. Two small grille pieces beside the main grille continued the theme. The area directly below these grilles was painted flat black. Except for modified mounting receptacles for the 1973 and later drain pan, these pieces were never modified. The grille material was different on the 916 and 914-6 GT and covered about twice the territory for improved cooling.

Rear grille with gold letter set

1974 silver plastic rear letter set

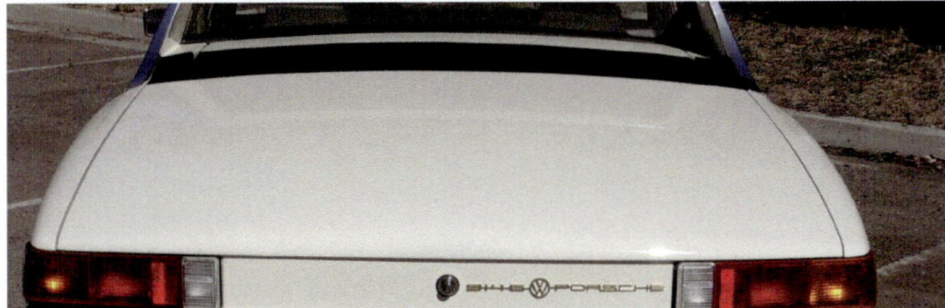

European spec. 914s had no lettering on the rear grille

Rear grille, 916

On US specification cars the word PORSCHE was on the center section of the grille. This was in the form of the individual letters that were used on rear lids of 911s. Gold-anodized aluminum letters were used from 1970 through 1972, with 1973 cars having bright-anodized letters. Chrome-plated plastic letters were used from 1974 through 1976. Cars not destined for our shores had no such grille adornment; nor did the 914-6 GT or 916.

Four-cylinder cars had a plastic tray installed to the lower part of the engine lid below the grille to protect the engine and electrical components from inclement weather. It was modified in 1973 from a plain tray, which hooked to the lid, to a ribbed tray, which bolted to the lid. Trays were not fitted on the 914-6 (*see photo page 36*).

Early style rear grille drain tray

Late ribbed drain tray

Taillight, US

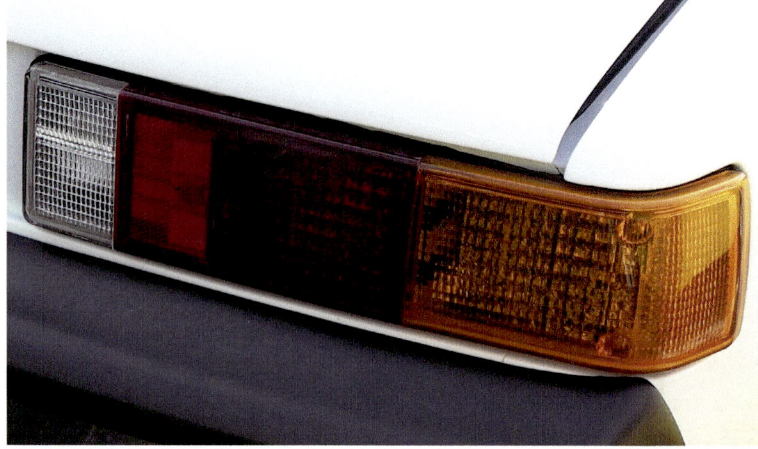

Taillight, Euro

Tail Panel

The tail panel, running across the car above the rear bumper, was the home of the taillights, rear scripts and rear trunk release.

The shape of the Hella taillight unit allowed the side reflector to be included in the portion that wrapped around the side. From outside to inside, the lens on US cars had a red side marker, red turn signal and taillight lens and a red reflector. At the inside was a clear back-up light. 914s built for the rest of the world did not have the side reflector built into the outer turn signal lens. French-specification cars had an amber turn signal, a red taillight, a red reflector and a yellow back-up light. All other countries had an amber turn signal, a red taillight, a red reflector and a clear back-up light. No modifications were made during production.

Rear fog lights were available as options on non-US 914s of all vintages. These were small square light units used on contemporary 911s which mounted to the left side of the tail panel on the right of the taillight. A special bracket was made specifically for the 914 allowing this light to be fitted.

The 914 carried a model-designation script on the tail panel. These rear scripts again identified the US specification cars from all others. The 1970 through 1972 US cars had gold anodized aluminum scripts reading either 914 or 914-6 to the right of the trunk lid release. The rest of the world's 914s had scripts of the same material which read 914 VW PORSCHE or 914-6 VW PORSCHE. The 1972 916 had a totally different arrangement. On some examples the left script was the PORSCHE previously used on 1962 through 1965 356s. To its right was a small 916 (made from the European 914-6 script) followed by a small Porsche crest. On other 916s the 916 script was followed by a large 911 Porsche crest and then the PORSCHE script. Aside from prototype cars, these were the only uses of enameled Porsche emblems (except some 914-6 hub caps) on any 914. GTs had no scripts.

Through 1972, US spec. 4-cylinder cars had only this script

A rare combination, US spec.914-6 Sportomatic

Early Euro spec.4-cylinder sript

Euro version of the 914-6 script

One version of the 916 script

1973 1.7 script

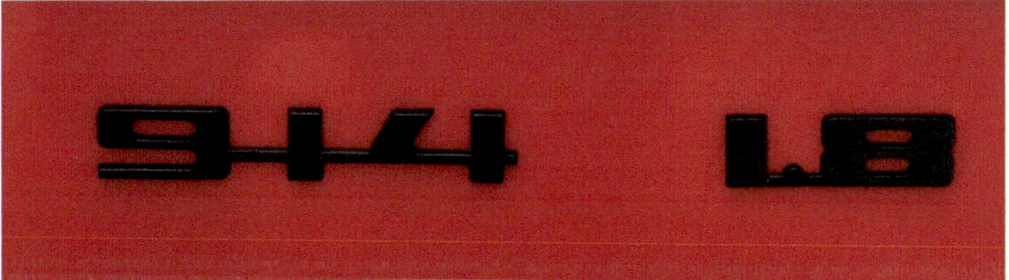

1974 914 and 1.8 scripts

Euro spec. 1974 2.0

The rear tunk lock was never changed

In 1973 the scripts became black to coordinate with other trim, but were still anodized aluminum. Non-US cars continued to use the familiar 914 VW PORSCHE script with US cars having 914. Since there were now two four-cylinder engines, scripts denoting displacement were supplied. These were to the right of the 914 script. In 1973 1.7 and 2.0 were made of black anodized aluminum.

In 1974 the 914, 2.0 and new 1.8 scripts were made of black plastic, although their size and general appearance were unaltered. This was likely a cost-saving move, as was the subsequent 1976 change to black adhesive vinyl. Non-US cars continued using the black aluminum VW Porsche script.

Rear bumper guards used in 1974

Rear bumper guards used on some US models 1975-1976

1973 914 and 2.0 scripts

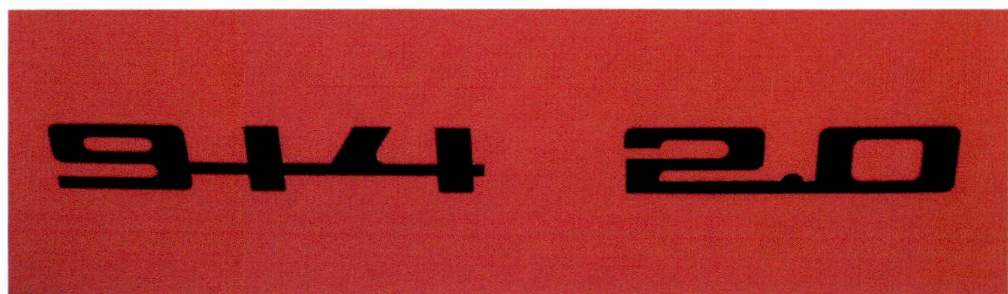

Vinyl decals, 1976

In the center of the tail panel was the cylindrical rear trunk lid release. Its lock was keyed to the door locks, ignition, glove box and luggage compartment locks.

Rear Bumper and Valance

The bumpers, caps and valances are discussed on pages 38 and 39. Other occupants include bumper guards, license lights and a towing eye access plug.

The first 914 rear bumper guards were similar to the front guards used on 1973 and 1974 US specification cars. These were used only in 914s destined for the US as 1974 models. These cars also had the additional bracing described on page 37. From 1975 on, California and Maryland-bound 914s had small rectangular extensions on the already impact absorbing-bumper. Some cars from other states, especially 1976 models, also have them.

The two varieties of license plate lights were both made by Hella. The first type was fitted to the lower edge of the urethane bumper cap

License light 1970-1974

License light 1975-1976

Tow hook plugs: chrome-plated, painted and synthetic rubber

Original rear license plate bracket

piece. Two lights mounted in tandem lit the license plate below. The impact-absorbing bumper of 1975 had different license lights, also found on 1974 and later 911s. They were located to either side of the plate in the center recess.

In the bumper, below the rear reflector on the driver's side was a small round plastic plug covering a threaded receptacle that could accept the towing eye in the tool kit. The plugs followed the progression of bumper finish and revision, i.e. body color, chrome and black. The only substantial change was for the 1975 crash bumper, when the size changed, as did the material to synthetic rubber.

Mud flaps for the rear wheels to keep debris from accumulating in the jack receiver area were available from 1970 through 1976. A change in mounting bracket is noted for the 1973 model year corresponding to the introduction of the short valance.

Wheels and Hub Caps

Except on the 914-6 and 4-cylinder cars with the appearance group, 4 ½ x 15" Volkswagen, silver-painted steel wheels were standard equipment through 1972. In 1973 a modification allowed the wheel to be centered on the hub (rather than the lug bolts). External appearance was similar, but the wheel was an inch wider. Both of these wheels had a chrome-plated center cap. The non-US cars received standard Volkswagen hub caps complete with VW emblems, while US cars had similar caps with no emblems. Lug bolts were standard steel ones used on the Volkswagen 411.

From 1974 through 1976 the standard wheel was steel and again from Volkswagen origins. These 5½ x 15" wheels were easily identified by the large *X* in the center pressing. They were more inset than the Volkswagen version due to the tighter fender clearance. A flat black cap covered the center hole. Lug bolts on these wheels were concealed by black plastic covers with domed tops.

Optional wheel types on the four cylinder cars included one 5½ x 15" steel wheel and three 5½ x 15" alloy wheels. The optional steel wheel, unlike the standard 4½" wheel, does not have a Volkswagen part number. It was similar in appearance to the standard wheel, only more deeply offset. It was first offered as part of the appearance group trim package in 1970. A modification for the self-centering hub was made in 1973. Both used the same hub caps as the standard wheel.

For the 1970 through 1973 four-cylinder cars, an aluminum alloy wheel manufactured by Pedrini was offered as an option. It featured eight cooling slots and an *X* pattern was made by alternating ribs with the remaining ribs running from the rim to the lug bolts (see photo). The 1973 Pedrini wheels had a larger center hole machined for the revised hubs. Special (and expensive) cadmium-plated steel lug bolts were used with this and subsequent alloy wheels. A small stainless steel cap without manufacturer's emblem covered the center of the wheel.

In 1973 all 2.0 914s with appearance group option package received a new four-spoke forged wheel made by Fuchs. There was some

Steel 4½" wheel with US-style hub cap

Steel 5½" wheel with Euro-style VW hub cap

1974-1976 Steel 5½" wheel

Optional Pedrini aluminum alloy wheel

Optional forged Fuchs alminum alloy wheel

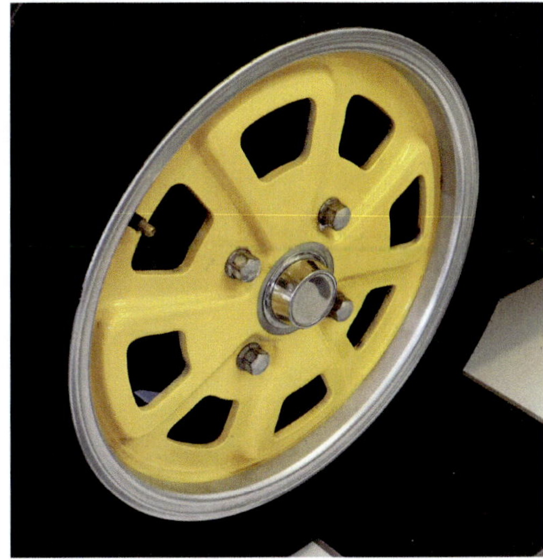

Unusual factory painted Fuchs wheel

family resemblance to the Fuchs forged wheel that was widely used on the 911. From 1974 through 1976 this wheel was optional for all other 914s. The same lug bolts and center caps were used as on the Pedrini wheels.

Also in 1973, the final type of aluminum alloy wheel was introduced. This wheel, made by Mahle, was similar to the earlier Pedrini wheel but had eight equal-length spokes and larger cooling holes. In 1973, they were used on 2.0 cars without the appearance group option

Left to right, 914-4: alloy wheel bolt, steel wheel bolt, plastic bolt cover 914-6: steel lug nut, aluminum alloy wheel lug nut

package. When fitted to 1974 Limited Edition cars, the wheel center was painted to match the valances, rockers and side stripes. Otherwise, these wheels were painted silver. They were optional equipment from 1974 through 1976 and shared the lug bolts and caps of the other alloy wheels.

Standard on the 914-6 were silver-painted 5½ x 15" steel wheels. These were the same wheels found on 911s. They used 911 stainless steel hubcaps with *tarnished chrome* or enameled Porsche crests. As an option, the wheels could be ordered in chrome finish.

The three following optional wheels for the 914-6 were also 911 options. The cast magnesium 10-spoke 5½ x 15" wheel manufactured by Mahle was also optional on 1969 through 1972 911Ts. Weighing in at ten pounds, this was the lightest wheel ever used on a production Porsche. Another option was the 5½ x 14" Fuchs forged alloy wheel fitted to the contemporary 911E. With the M471 option package, 6 x 15" Fuchs wheels were fitted at each corner. Wheel spacers (21 mm) were also fitted, as were longer lugs.

All three wheels utilized the same aluminum cap as the 911. Lug nuts on steel wheels were steel; alloy and magnesium wheels used aluminum nuts.

Painted centers were found on Limited Edition 914s

Steel 5½" 914-6 wheel with tarnished-chrome cap

The very light Mahle gas burner 914-6 wheel

Fuchs 5½ x 14" wheel

Fuchs 6 x 15" wheel

Fuchs 7 x 15" wheel

Fuchs 8 x 15" GT wheel

The wheels on the 914-6 GT and 916 were again forged Fuchs alloys. The 916 had 7 x 15" at all four corners, while GTs generally had the 7 x 15" front and 8 x 15" rear. The 916 center cap and aluminum lug nuts were the same as those used with the 914-6 alloy wheels.

Luggage Compartments

Front Luggage Compartment

By virtue of its mid-engine design, the 914 featured luggage space fore and aft. Both afforded a goodly amount of usable space, with the rear trunk able to stow the top, as well. The principle contents of the front luggage compartment were the fuel tank, the spare wheel, the air conditioner condenser (dealer installed), the windshield washer system and the tool kit.

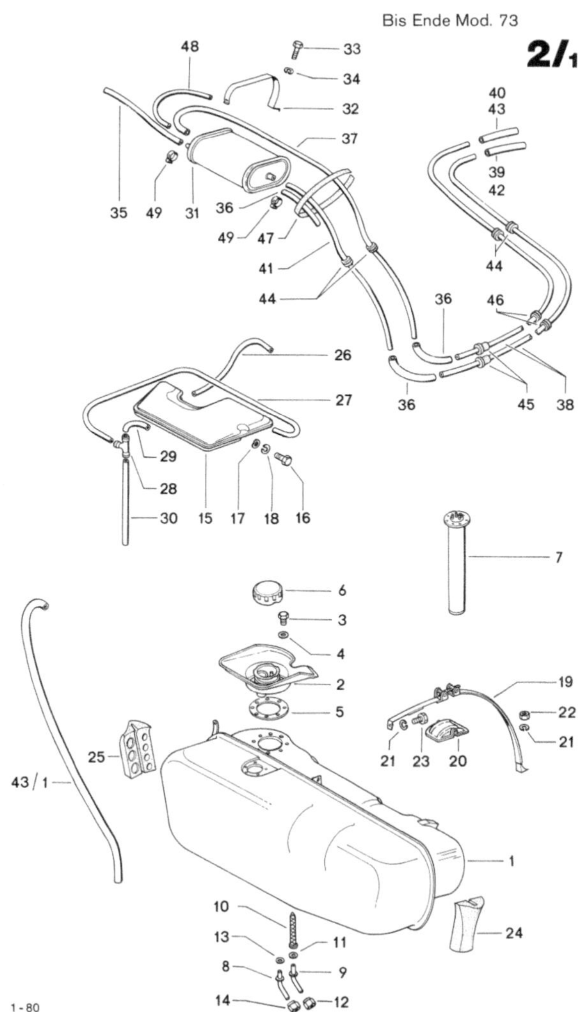

Illustration 2/1

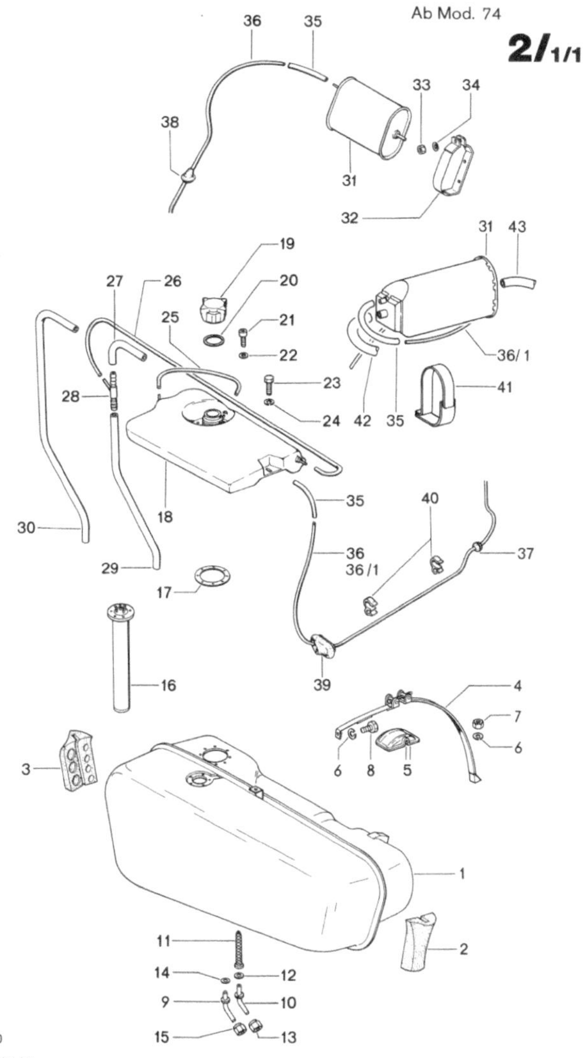

Illustration 2/1/1

Fuel Tank

By the 1970s, pollution regulating agencies such as the US Environmental Protection Agency, had made fuel tanks complicated mazes of tubing and evaporation chambers. As can be seen in illustrations 2/1 and 2/1/1, the 914 was no exception. The fuel tank was essentially the same through mid-1974 and had a capacity of 16.4 gallons. Its

Fuel tank 1970 914-6

Fuel tank 1971 914-4 with carbon canister

filler was reached by opening the front hood, similar to its 356 fore-runners. A silver clip-on gas cap was surrounded by a steel expansion reservoir on three sides. Starting in 1971 US cars were equipped with a carbon filtration device for fuel vapor. The fuel tank was cushioned by rubber supports on each side with three carpet strips underneath and secured by a strap in the center. Four and six-cylinder cars shared the same tank.

The later tank, first installed in April/May 1974, was similar. It used the same rubber supports, mounting strap and electrical sending unit. The most obvious difference was that the fuel filler was now in the plastic expansion chamber. The revised gas cap was black plastic

Japan spec. early 1974 tank without carbon canister

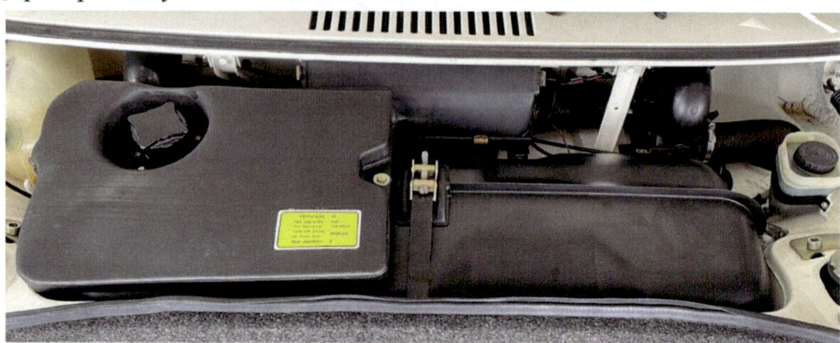

The late 1974 fuel tank

and unscrewed. California models got their own unique expansion chamber for 1975 with restrictive filler hole, since these cars were catalyst equipped and used unleaded fuel.

On 1971-1973 models the carbon canister rested on top of the fuel tank on the left side. The canister was modified November/December 1973 and was moved to the engine compartment.

On some of the 914-6 GT cars built for long distance events, a larger 26.4 gallon foam-filled (for safety) fuel tank was installed. Installation required removal of the front chassis bulkhead and use of a reinforcing bar mounted between the strut towers.

1975-1976 49-state US spec. fuel tank

1975-1976 California fuel tank with unleaded fuel sticker

Carbon filtration canisters were developed by Volkswagen

Large 26.4 gallon GT fuel tank

Windshield Washer System and Brake Fluid Reservoir

Nestled next to the fuel tank on the passenger side was the windshield washer reservoir. Four and six-cylinder cars differed in this area. The six had the same electric pump used in the 911, operated by the same steering column stalk. Instead of an electric pump, the four drew its power from air pressure in the spare tire, like Volkswagens. The latter incorporated a pressure valve which did not allow the tire to go below safe driving pressure.

The fluid reservoirs of the four and the six were similar in size and shape. Due to different operating methods the similarity ended there. The one on the 914-6 had inlet and output tubes entering at a single location on top of the reservoir. The four had the inlet (pressure) line through the filler cap and the output through a separate aperture on the reservoir's bottom.

Tubing and T-fittings were the same as used on contemporary 911s, as shown in illustrations 9/5 (914-6) and 9/5/1 (four-cylinder models). Washer nozzles are described on page 45, and switches are described on pages 69, 72-73.

To the left of the fuel tank, above the driver's feet, was the brake master cylinder reservoir. The master cylinders on four and six-cylinder cars differed only in bore (17 mm on the four and 19 mm on the 914-6) and could be interchanged.

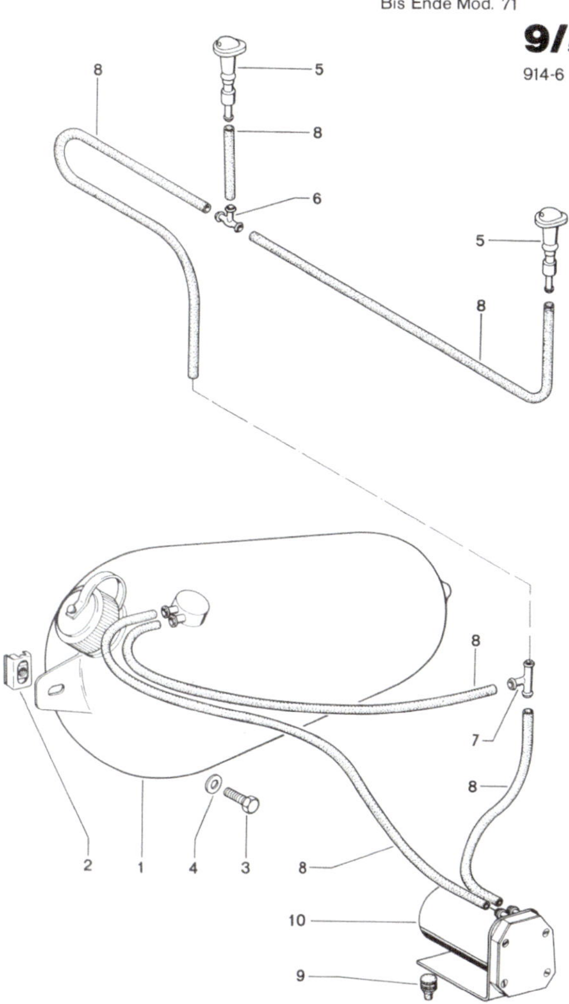

Illustration 9/5

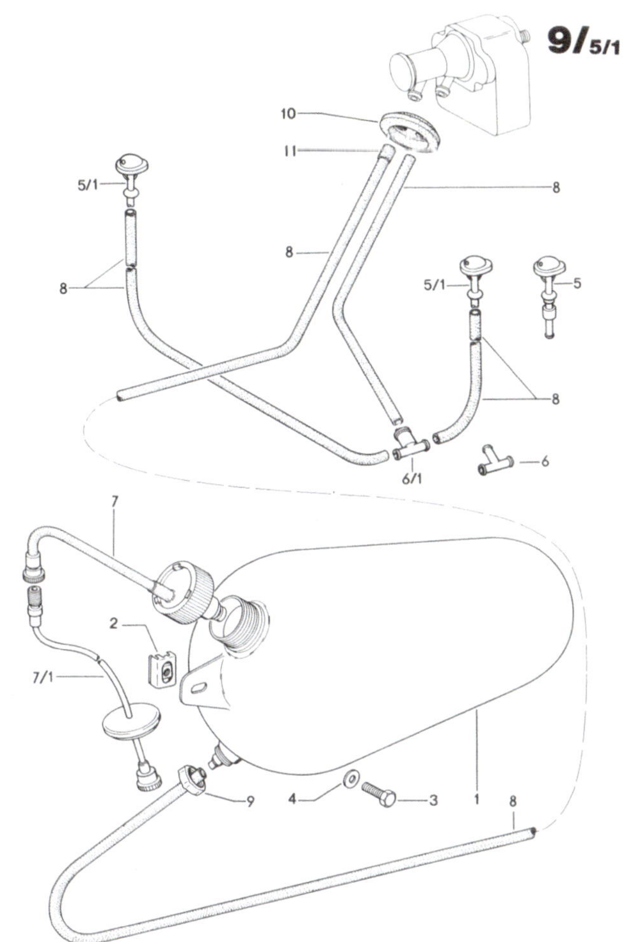

Illustration 9/5/1

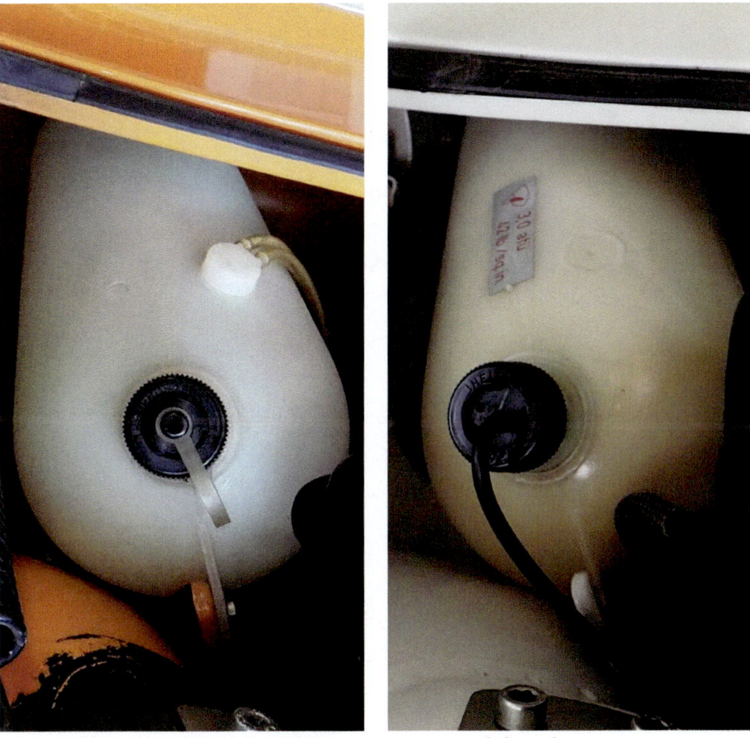

Electrically operated 914-6 washer system reservoir, left and air pressure operated four-cylinder reservoir, right

Air line from washer bottle attached to the upside down-mounted spare tire

Spare Wheel Area, Tool Kit

Spare wheels on all production 914s matched the wheels on each corner of the car. They were positioned with the *A-side* down. Above the spare was a carpeted cover. The gray felt carpet matched the piece of carpeting covering the front of the partition separating the luggage space from the fuel tank. The cover was modified to fit the reshaped nose panel in 1975, when the bumper change occurred. Some prototype cars had the fuel tank area covered by carpet as well, but this was not carried into production versions. The 916 had carpet-covered sidewalls, inner nose and headlight boxes in addition to the carpet found on standard 914s. The 916 also had a space-saver spare

Carpet-covered platform covered the spare tire

A notch was cut in the front of the spare tire cover to allow clearance for the lower front latch when dealer-installed air conditioning was installed

The brake master cylinder reservoir used on all 914s

mounted to the vertical partition between the fuel tank and luggage area.

Tool kits were generally found in the center of the spare tire. As would be expected, the kits for the four and six-cylinder cars were different.

The 914-6 kit contained:

Bag, basket-weave vinyl
Spark plug wrench
19 mm wheel nut wrench
Allen wrench for oil drain plug
8 x 9 mm open-end wrench
10 x 11 mm open-end wrench
12 x 13 mm open-end wrench
14 x 15 mm open-end wrench
17 x 19 mm open-end wrench
19 x 22 mm box wrench
Screwdriver (red plastic handle)
Phillips screwdriver (red plastic handle)
Pliers
Fan belt
Plastic bag with fuses
Towing eye

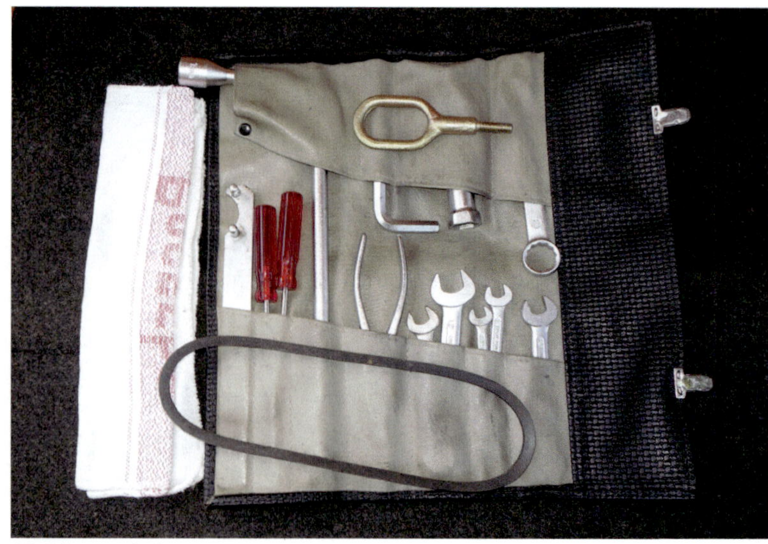
Tool kit, 914-6

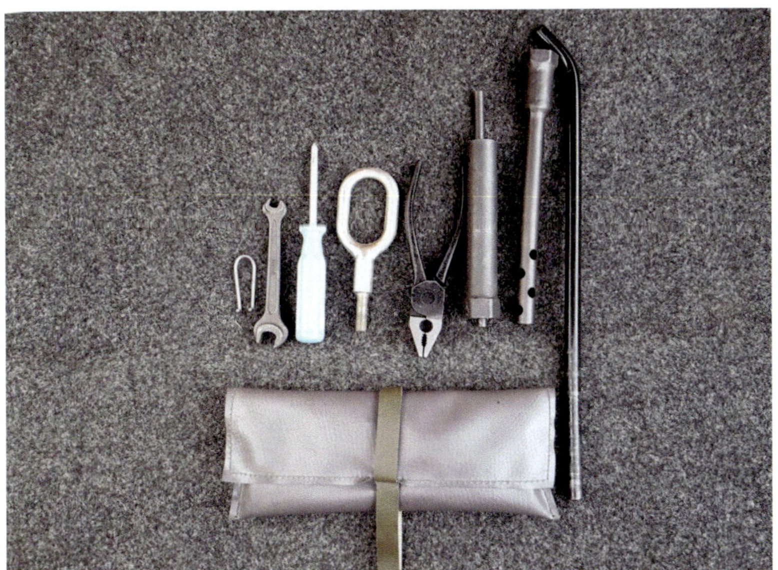
Tool kit, 1970-1973 914-4

1970 through early 1973 914 four-cylinder tool kits contained:

Bag, gray vinyl
Socket wrench for wheel bolts
Socket wrench for spark plugs
Tommy bar for wheel wrench
Tommy bar for plug wrench
8 x 13 mm open-end wrench
Phillips/slotted combination screwdriver
Hub cap removal tool
Towing eye

Casually installed VPC condenser with tire mounting bracket

DPD condenser with tire-mounting cone

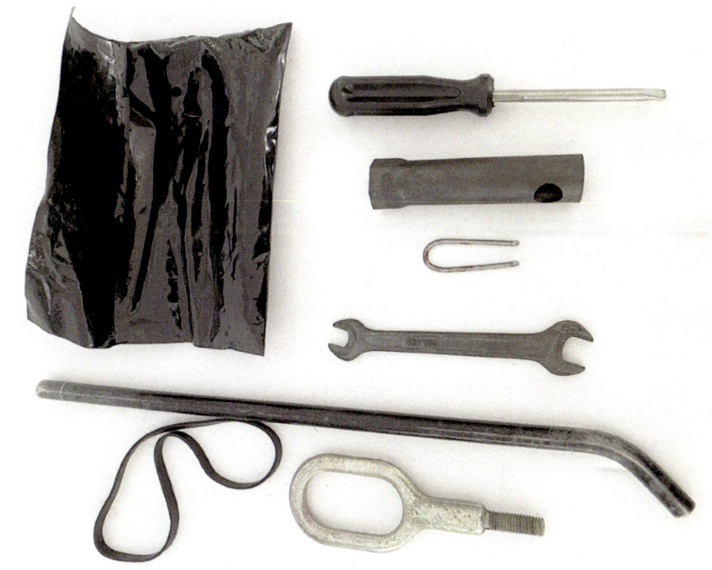
Revised tool kit from mid-1973

Mid-1973 and later tool kits contained:

Bag, black plastic, secured with black rubber band
Socket wrench for wheel bolts and spark plugs
Tommy bar for socket wrench
10 x 13 mm open-end wrench
Phillips/slotted combination screwdriver
Hub cap removal tool
Towing eye

The final occupant in the spare tire area was the condenser for the air conditioner. Since all air conditioners were dealer installed, some differences are common. Installation was performed by cutting a rectangular hole in the floor and bolting the condenser in place.

The two companies that provided air conditioning units for the US market were DPD Manufacturing Company, Inc. and VPC (Volkswagen Products Corporation). The DPD condenser had a plastic cone-shaped cover that centered the spare wheel (A-side up). The VPC condenser had a metal bracket on top to which the spare tire was bolted using the standard hold-down hardware.

The 916 had more extensive carpeting and front-mounted oil cooler

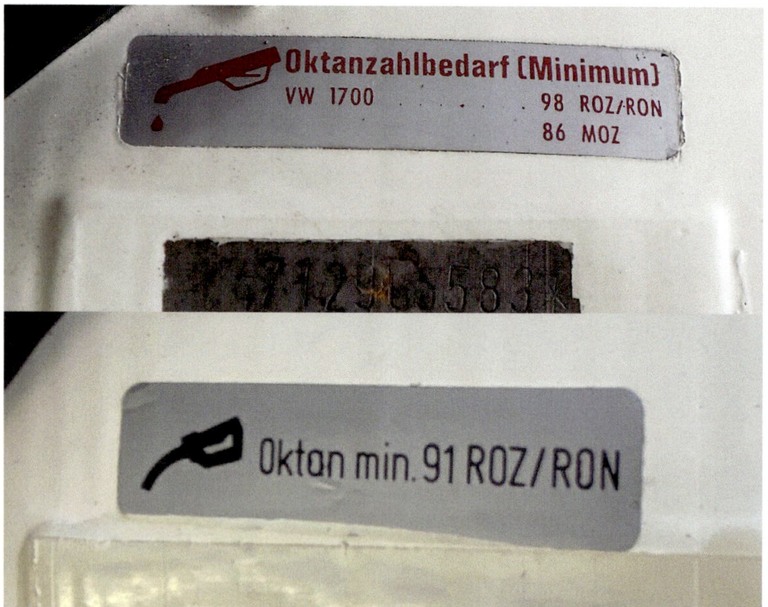

Early red (1970-1972) and late black (1973-1976) US spec. octane stickers

Stickers

Above the stamped chassis number on the right side wheel house was a silver-colored octane requirement sticker on all four-cylinder US spec. 914s. From 1970-1972 the type was red and included the words *VW 1700*. The sticker used from 1973-on had black graphics.

Gold-colored foil tire pressure/capacity stickers were first found on the fuel tank expansion tank of US. spec. four-cylinder models in 1972. Prior to that they were located in the engine compartment (*see pages 97-98*). There were two different versions based on the wheel width fitted. There were again two different stickers for 1973 based on wheel size, which featured reduced vehicle capacity from 705 to 550 lbs. The 1974 version was unchanged, though 4½" wide wheels were eliminated along with the sticker for those. They did not change with the new style fuel tank mid-1974.

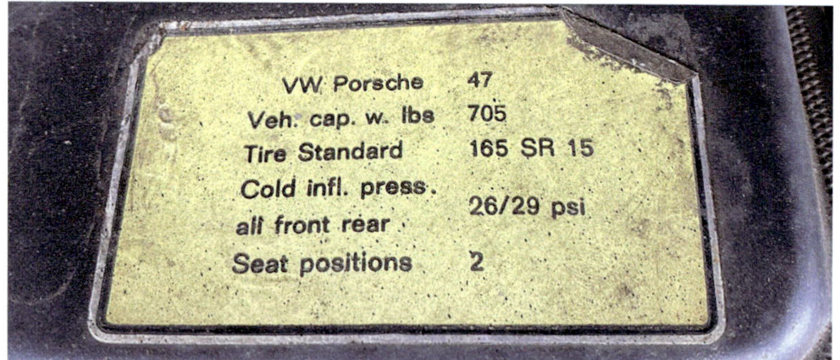

1972 sticker for car fitted with 5½" wide wheels

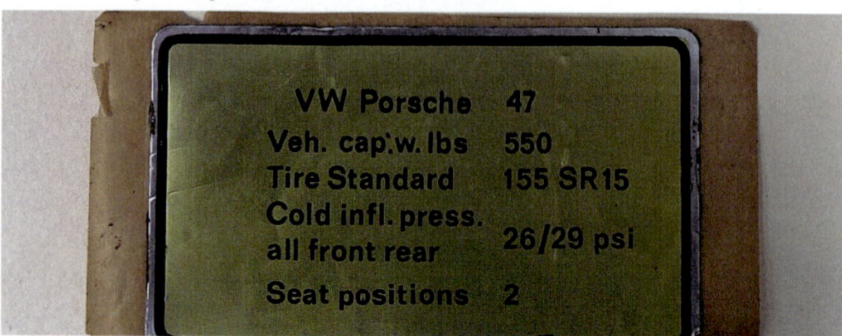

1973 sticker for car fitted with 4½" wide wheels

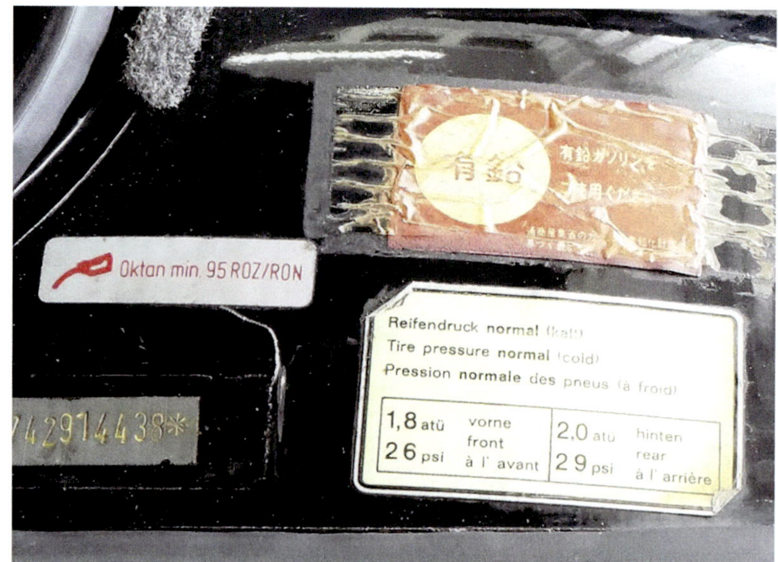

Japanese spec. 1974 Limited Edition has a higher octane red version of the 1973-1976 octane sticker and tire pressure sticker used on the 1969-1971 911. It had no sticker on the fuel tank

In 1975 a different silver-colored sticker with black lettering was located in the same place on the fuel tank. There were once again two versions supplied for US spec. models. The only difference was the designation of SR rated tires for 1.8 models and HR tires for 2.0s.

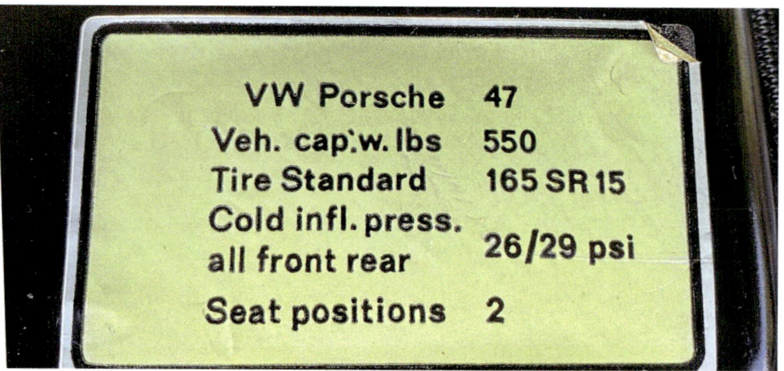

1973-1974 sticker for car fitted with 5½" wide wheels

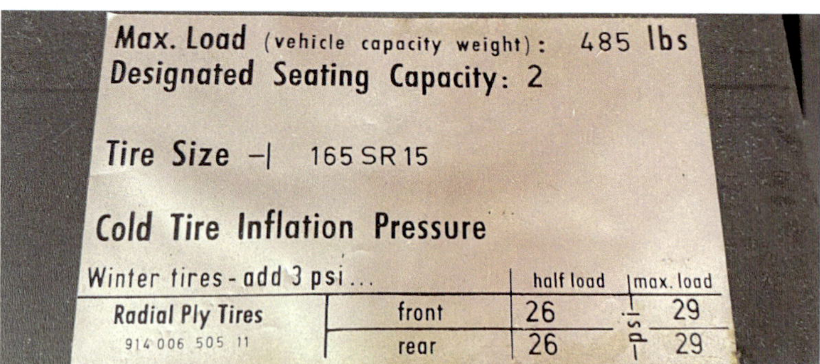

1975-1976 sticker for car fitted with 1.8 engine

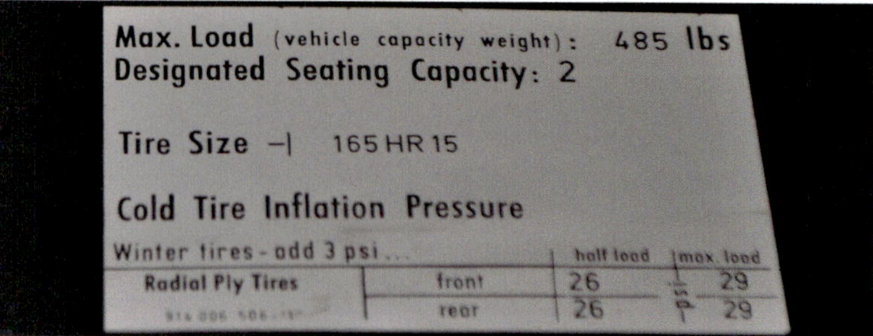

1975-1976 sticker for car fitted with 2.0 engine

A threaded receptacle was used to secure the spare tire in the rear compartment

Later rear compartment area with jack at front under carpet

We have insufficient data about cars produced for other markets. 914-6 models did not have any stickers in the front luggage area.

Rear Trunk Compartment

The rear trunk compartment was fairly shallow, since the transmission and suspension components were below. Covering the floor was gray felt molded carpet identical to that found in the front compartment. The carpet was modified 1/1/72 when the jack was moved from the left rear inner fender to directly below the luggage compartment light. The 916 also had carpeted side walls and tail panel.

1973 through mid-1974 had this thick foam pad

Early rear compartment with jack mounted on left side

The 916 had carpet on all side walls

In 1970-1972 there was a small foam pad under the carpet above the muffler. 1973 through mid-1974 had a thick foam pad covering the entire luggage area. A final variety, used from around February 1974 also covered the entire area, but was made from a black plastic-covered foam, modified due to problems associated with water accumulation.

Small foam pad used from 1970-1972

The final plastic-covered foam rear pad

1970-early 1974 rear top mounts were mounted with bolts, later ones with rivets

Illuminating the rear trunk was a single light unit identical to the license plate light used on 911s through 1973. It was mounted on the forward wall of the compartment slightly left of center. This light remained on whenever the car's headlights or running lights were on, since there was no lid-triggered switch to control it.

The rear trunk compartment was also designed to hold the top which was placed in such a way to minimize reduction of luggage space. The top's forward edge was secured by white plastic clips (which often broke with use) that were initially secured with bolts then changed to rivets in February/March 1974. In the rear, the top was held by two rubber clips, sided left and right, which also often broke with use.

Rubber shock top cover, plastic well and rear compartment light

Toward the front of the rear trunk were two round white plastic wells just forward of each shock tower. These accommodated the front top mounting brackets, allowing them to remain undamaged when storing the top. The shock towers had rubber cones concealing the top mount. These parts did not change during production.

The jack was stored in the rear trunk compartment. From 1970 through December 1971 a resistance lever-type jack was found on the driver's side, toward the rear. It was secured by a metal clamp and rested on a small piece of carpet. From January 1972, a crank-type jack was located under the luggage compartment light and held in place by rubber strap.

Rubber rear top mount. Note electrical relay for catalyst-equipped exhaust probe

The top was designed to be stowed in the rear compartment

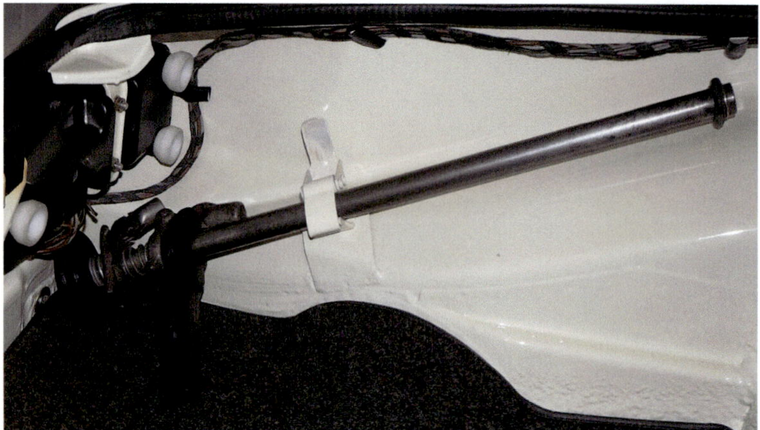

Rear-mounted resistance jack 1970-December 1971

Crank type jack used from January 1972

Interior

Dashboard

The 914 was the first production Porsche since 1955 to feature a removable dashboard. The steel framework for the dashboard (*illustration 8/11, number 10*) of four and six-cylinder cars differed because the ignition and wiper switches varied between the two. A third version of the dash was used on all models from 1972 on. This corresponds to the wiper/washer system controls being moved to the column on four-cylinder cars, disappearance of the center defroster vent and the appearance of fresh air vents on the ends of the dashboard.

The dashboard was capped by a single piece of molded self-skinning black urethane. The grain on the dash top matched the smooth vinyl grain used on the 1972-1974 seats. The four-cylinder cars had three defroster vents; the 914-6 lacked the center vent because the higher volume of cooling air from the six-cylinder engine made the central vent unnecessary. Changes in the dashboard cap occurred at the 1972 and 1973 model year. The 1972 change was due to the addition of side vents and loss of central defroster vent. The 1973 change was the use of a lever adjuster which replaced the earlier thumb roller on the side vents. The 916 had a leather dash covering, color coded to the upholstery.

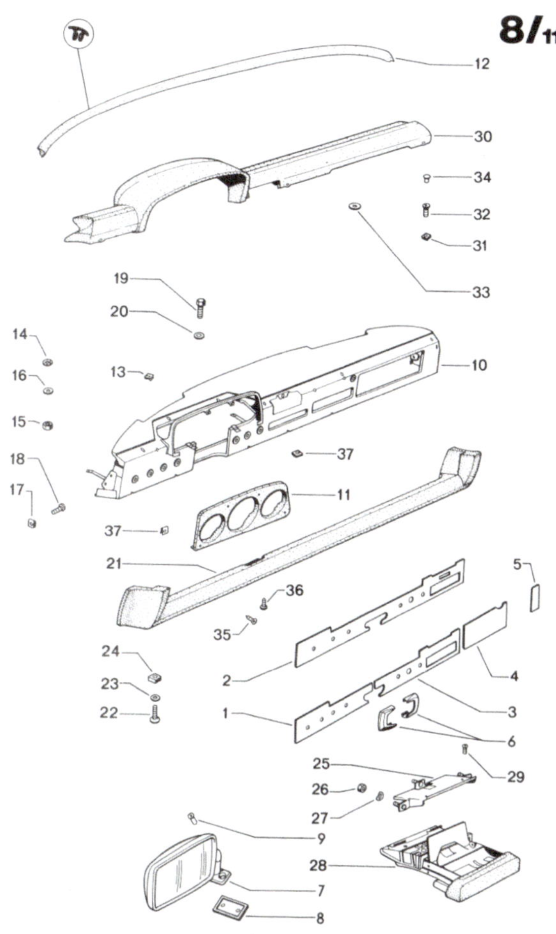

Illustration 8/11

A center defroster vent was only found on 4-cylinder cars in 1970-1971

The 914-6 lacked the center defroster vent

The final dash top configuration used from 1973

Leather-wrapped 916 dashboard

Between this cap and the windshield was a vinyl-covered foam and a rubber seal. The ashtray was recessed into the cap piece just to the right of the instrument pod. The ashtray and seal were not altered during production.

Surrounding the three main instruments was a black steel panel which held the gauges. For 1975-1976 it was changed to plastic. This panel was interchangeable on four and six-cylinder cars.

Instruments

All 914s had three large instruments directly in front of the driver. They were, from left to right, combination fuel level gauge, tachometer and speedometer. All were held in place by press-in rubber sealing rings shared with contemporary 911s. These instruments had black faces, white calibrations and red-orange indicator needles.

The centrally-mounted ash tray was unchanged 1970-1976

Metal instrument surround panel on 1971 914-4 with early fuel gauge

One of only eleven Crayford right-hand-drive conversions from the UK

The combination instrument on the 914-6 was unique to that model with an oil temperature scale at the top and a fuel level indicator below. Warning lights were aligned in a row between the two, left to right: oil pressure (green), handbrake (red), Sportomatic oil temperature (red or white and non-functional on cars not equipped with Sportomatic transmissions) and generator (red). This gauge had a silver button in the middle to match the tach and speedometer.

The 1970 four-cylinder 914s had a left-side gauge with the top having a large red handbrake warning light with the fuel gauge below. The red warning light on the right was for the generator function and on the left was a green oil pressure light. Shortly into the 1971 model year in October/November 1970, the warning lights were reversed, though the rest of the gauge was the same. A silver button was located in the center to match the other two instruments.

Combination gauge 914-6

Second version of the left side 914-4 fuel gauge had warning lights reversed

Fuel gauge 1974-1976 equipped with center console

Fuel gauge 1974-1976 without center console

Combination gauge, 916

1973 through early 1974 cars had a similar instrument as used in the 1971 and 1972 cars with two warning lights as above and could be ordered with an optional temperature scale on top and fuel scale below. Warning lights from left to right on the gauge with temperature scale: oil pressure (green), handbrake (red), blank (white), and generator (red). It also had the silver button in the center.

By March 1974 through 1976 all 914s had a different gauge that was similar in appearance to the earlier version with two warning lights, but had no button in the center and a shorter bezel. Warning lights for the version with the temperature gauge, from left to right: handbrake (red), generator (red), blank (white), and oil pressure (green).

The 916 used a 911 gauge with oil temperature scale on the left and oil pressure scale on the right. It had a red brake warning light at the top and a red generator light at the bottom.

The electronic tachometer was centrally located and was the largest of the three instruments at 115 mm diameter. The diameter of the two gauges flanking it was 100 mm. The 914-6, because it had two more cylinders, did not share tachometers with other 914s, though it was specific to that model. On the other hand, the 916 used a 911 tach which corresponded to the engine installed. The 914-6 GT featured higher 10,000 RPM calibration corresponding to the higher-revving race engine. Tachs in these cars were generally turned so that the shift point was at the top.

Tachometer 914-6

Tachometer early 914-4

916 tachometer was calibrated to the engine installed

10,000 RPM GT tachometer with no red line

Later 4-cylinder tachometer with revised center button and indicator lights

California 1976 tachometer with accompanying emissions warning lights

Through early-1974 all four-cylinder cars, regardless of displacement, used one tachometer. The indicator needle center button was silver. The one used from at least March 1974 had a black center button. At the top of the early tach were two arrow-shaped green turn signal indicator lights. A single round turn indicator light was found on the later gauge with the black button. The early tach had a blue high beam indicator at the bottom, while it was moved to the upper right on the later gauge.

The speedometer was to the right of the tachometer. All speedometers had both regular and trip odometers. They also had a green parking light indicator at the bottom center.

The 914-6 models used two different speedometers. For mile countries a 150-mph unit was fitted, while everyone else received a 250-kph instrument. Both of these were shared with the 911, not unique to the 914-6 as with the other two gauges.

The four-cylinder cars used no fewer than eight different speedometers. There were two 120-mph and two 200-kph units used prior to the 1973 model introduction. One of each pair was calibrated for use with 155 x 15 tires; the other pair was calibrated for 165 x 15 tires.

The 1973 1.7 liter 914 had the 200-kph unit used with 165 x 15 tires on earlier cars. In kilometer countries the 1973 2.0 liter 914s received a more optimistic 250-kph scale and all mile country 914s were upgraded to a 150-mph speedometer.

The final three speedometers were used from 1974-1976. They were a 150-mph gauge for mile countries, a 250-kph unit for kilometer countries and a special speedometer for Japan only. The latter had a warning buzzer that sounded at 100-kph. Like the other instruments, the center buttons were silver initially and black from around March 1974.

914-6 150-mph speedometer

Early 914-4 120-mph speedometer

Late 914-4 150-mph speedometer

914-6 250-kph speedometer

Early 914-4 200-kph speedometer

1974 Japanese spec. 250-kph speedometer

Center console-mounted clock

1973 center console-mounted temperature gauge

1974-on center console-mounted temperature gauge

Center console-mounted voltmeter

US-spec. 916 with air-conditioning, fuel gauge/clock

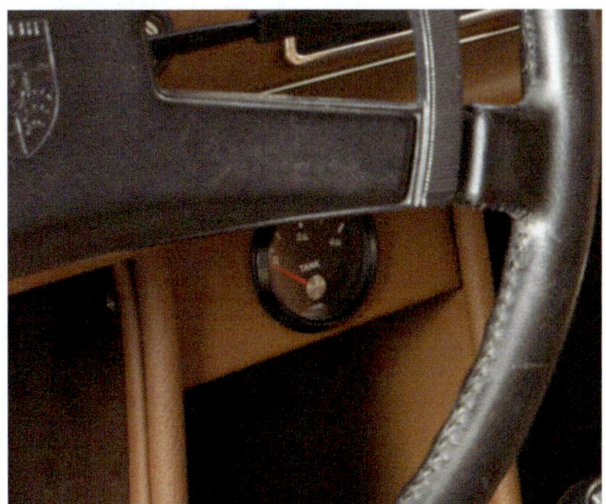
Euro spec. 916 had console with fuel gauge

Optional Instruments

The 1973 and later 914s fitted with appearance group center consoles had three optional VDO gauges in vertical orientation. Topmost was a clock, with an oil temperature gauge below and at the bottom, a voltmeter. These were standard on all 1973 2.0 models and optional on all 1974-1976 cars. Only the oil temperature gauge changed and that was for the 1974 model year. The difference consisted of altering the position of the red area on the hot part of the scale (*see photos above*).

The 916 did not have the large console found on the 1973 and later models, but rather had a smaller center deposit box fitted with a solitary fuel level gauge at the top. The only US specification 916 which was fitted with air conditioning and had a fuel gauge and clock mounted below.

Switches and Dashboard-Mounted Controls

Following the 914's introduction in 1969, a number of motoring publications criticized its rather Spartan interior. Some remarked negatively about the use of familiar Volkswagen switches. With the exception of the indicators on the 914-6 steering column and the heater controls, all were at least partially period Volkswagen.

The headlight switch was on the left. It was a Porsche switch with a Volkswagen knob. US specification 914s had different inserts with a light symbol. A change was made in the switch and knob at the 1972 model year, corresponding to a change allowing the headlight units to stay down when the parking lights were on. Another change occurred in 1974 pertaining to wiring related to the seatbelt interlock and warning buzzer, but did not alter the outward appearance.

The next switch to the right in 1970-1971 was the fog light switch for cars so equipped. From the 1972 model, the flasher was here and the fog light switch was to the right of it. Through 1972 the illuminated center was green in color. Later versions were gold-colored.

Left side switch cluster 1970 914-6

Euro-spec. 1971 914-6 with fog/driving lights did not have a switch for them

Left side switch cluster 1971 914-4

Left side switches 914-6 GT. Pull switches are for twin ignition coils

Euro-spec. models did not have this switch for the fitted auxiliary fog or driving lights. They automatically came on with the headlights.

The next switch was the four-way emergency flasher. US cars had a different switch with an additional pole so that the fog light switch could be grounded through it. The knob insert also differed between US and non-US cars. Both were standard Volkswagen parts, but the US version was more subtle. The flasher knob changed for the 1972 model year. It had the word *HAZARD* and a triangular symbol instead of the words *EMERGENCY 88 VW*.

Right side switch cluster 1970 914-6

Right side switch cluster 1972 914-6

Left side switch cluster 1974 Japanese-spec. 2.0. Note later switch order

1976 model without fog lights

On the 914-6 the ignition switch was next. This was a 911 part, complete with column lock, and for the US cars, a buzzer to let them know that the door was open and the key was still in the ignition. On four-cylinder cars the ignition switch was on the right of the steering column (*see page 73*).

On the right side of the steering column was another row of switches. The left one was the lighter. With the exception of the insert with symbol, the lighter was a Porsche-made part. It changed in 1973, as did all of the knobs, but the units could easily be exchanged. An accessory plug was available to insert into the lighter receptacle to power other 12-volt devices.

Right side switch cluster 1971 914-4

Right side switch cluster 1973 914-4

To the right of the lighter on the 914-6 and 1972-1976 914-4s was the rear window defogger on cars so equipped. It was the same switch and knob used for fog lights but had a different insert. This green-colored center was illuminated when in use. When this option was fitted on 1970-1971 four-cylinder cars, the switch was mounted to the left of the lighter.

Through 1971 four-cylinder cars had the windshield wiper switch on the dashboard as opposed to the column-mounted 914-6 switch. It was on the far right and the windshield washer was activated by pressing its center. In 1972 the wiper/washer control moved to the steering column (see *page 73*).

Cars with headlight washers had a rocker switch located to the upper left of the heater/blower control. This option was only available on 1974 through 1976 models, but never offered on US models.

Although the heater/blower control was similar to the one used on the 911, it was not the same part. The top lever regulated the amount of fresh air admitted to the interior. At the far right were the three blower settings in ascending order. The middle lever controlled the direction of fresh air; left was into the footwell, right was through the defroster and in the center, a combination of both. The bottom lever directed heated air in the same manner. The US cars had a light that indicated that the blower was on.

Heater/blower control, 1970-1972

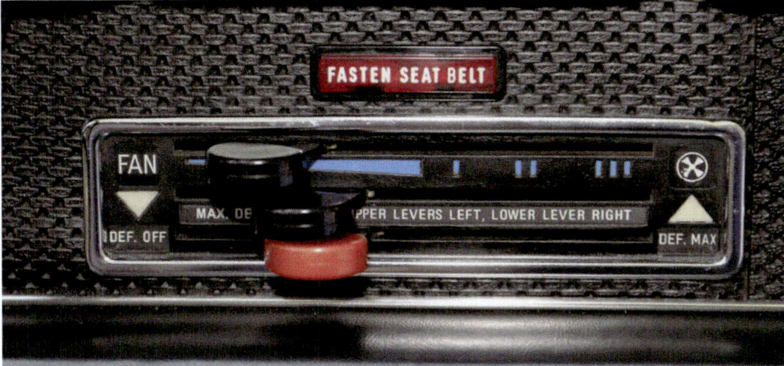

Heater/blower control, 1973-1974

Heater/blower control, 1975-1976

There were four different varieties of this control. The first was used from 1970-1971. The second, which was used only in 1972 had defrosting instructions written below the second lever in white with a red background. For 1973 and 1974, the instructions were on a black background and a the word *FAN* was in the upper left and a fan symbol was on the right. The final variety, 1975-1976 had black bezel. Earlier ones were chrome.

A final dashboard item was the *FASTEN SEAT BELT* warning light that was found above the blower control from 1972. It was modified to say *FASTEN BELTS* in 1975.

Lower Dash Trim

The vinyl insert for the lower dashboard was the same brick pattern material used for the 1972-1974 seat inserts. This material changed at the 1975 model year to a basket-weave pattern. It was always black in color. This material was glued to thin metal backing plates until 1975, when it became a one-piece vinyl/cardboard arrangement.

On the far right of the dashboard was the glove compartment. It had a simple locking door that pivoted up when opened. The glovebox and door were made smaller when the vents appeared in 1972. At the same time, the small plastic rectangular knob was replaced with a larger version.

Below and wrapping up the sides of the dashboard area was a panel made from the same black urethane as the dash top. This piece was changed at the

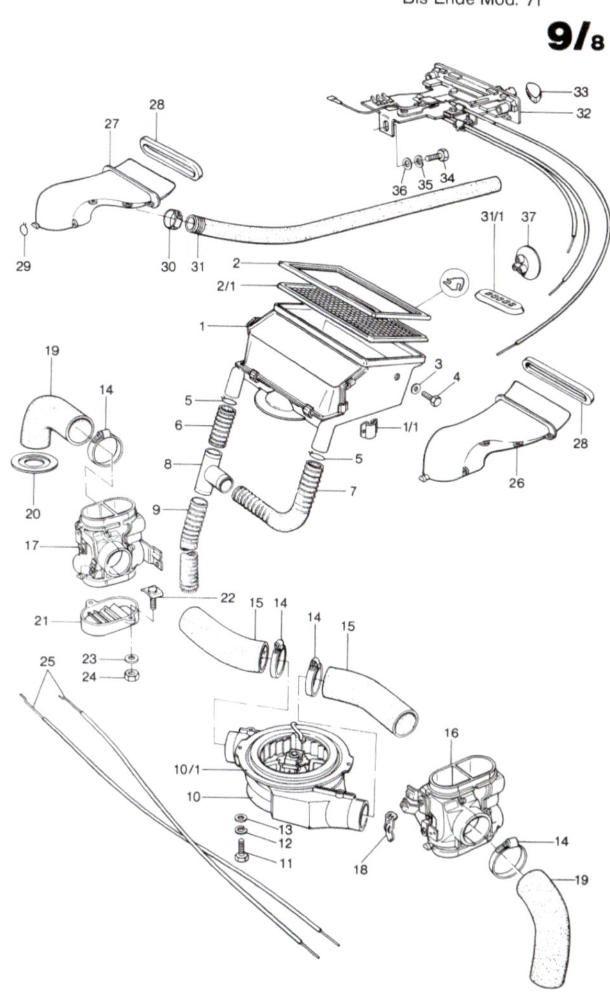

Illustration 9/8, 1970-1971 heater/defroster blower system

Glovebox was wider 1970-1971 prior to side vents

end of the 1971 model year and again March 1973. These changes correspond to the addition of side vents and their modification in mid-1973. The earlier type vent was directed side to side by a knurled knob, while the later one had a plastic lever.

Air conditioner controls and vents were in a plastic unit mounted directly below the dashboard. The differences between DPD and VPC units may be seen in the photos. Note also the modification to the center console when each type was installed.

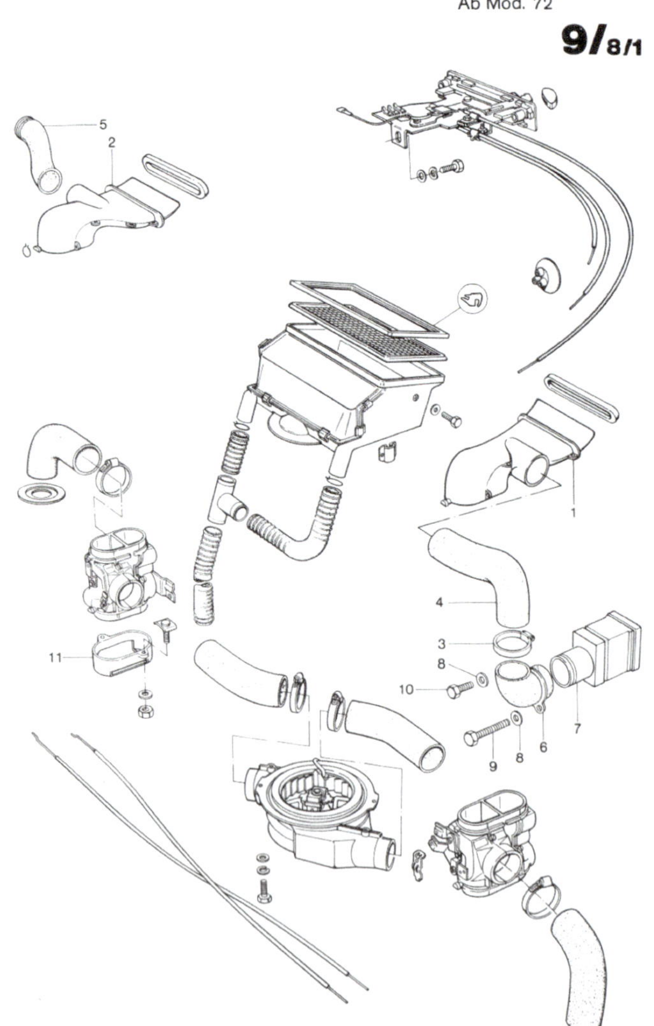

Illustration 9/8/1, 1972-1976 heater/defroster blower system with side vents

Glovebox from the 1972 model. Note revised knob

The hood release was just below the dashboard on the driver's side. This was a locking device that was unchanged throughout 914 production.

To the right of the hood release was the fuse block. It had a plastic cover with international symbols. The same fuse block was the same on all models and was never modified, although fuse amperage was.

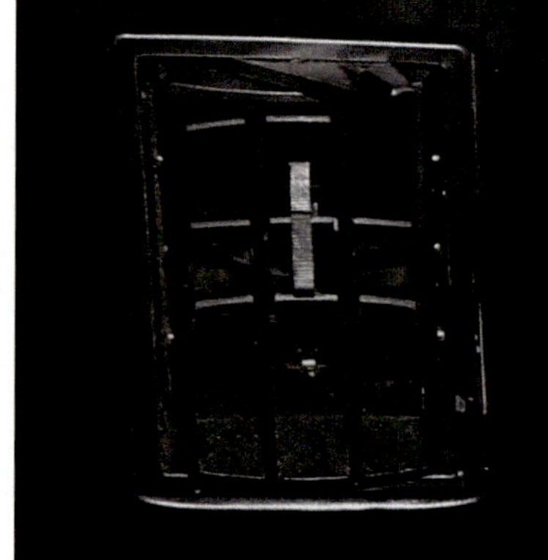

Side vent 1972 with knurled knob, left and mid-1973-1976 with lever, right

DPD air conditioning unit

VPC air conditioning unit

Locking front hood release

Under-dashboard fuse box

A blanking plate (left) was present when radio speaker was not fitted

Radio, Aerial

Radios, optional on all 914s, were located on the dashboard between the ventilation control and the glove box. On cars without radios, basket-weave upholstery covered this area.

Many radios were dealer-installed making numerous combinations of radios and aerials *original,* just not *factory.* The radio types offered as original equipment by the Porsche factory all were made by Blaupunkt, except for the Becker radios found in some 914-6s and 916s.

Radio speakers were located behind black plastic housings in each footwell. Different speakers were offered based on the radio fitted, but after prototype parts were used up, the housings were never changed. Blaupunkt made a special speaker with the magnet in the front due to the shallow compartment.

Factory-installed aerials were always on the left front fender close to the cowl area. They were made by Hirschmann and had a bright finish. Power antennas could not be fitted due to insufficient clearance under the front fender. As mentioned on page 32, the 916 aerial was imbedded in the windshield glass.

Blaupunkt Frankfurt US

Becker Europa radio would have been dealer or owner installed

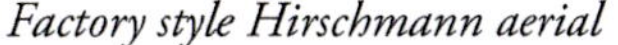

Factory style Hirschmann aerial

Dealer-installed Bosch blue-tip aerial

FACTORY INSTALLED RADIOS

1970

914-4

Blaupunkt
Wolfsburg, AM/LW
Wolfsburg - US, AM
Emden, AM/FM/LW
Emden - US, AM/FM

914-6

Blaupunkt
Boston, AM (US band)
Frankfurt, AM/FM/LW/SW
Frankfurt - US, AM/FM
Köln, AM/FM/LW signal seeking
New York, AM/FM/SW signal seeking (US band)

Becker
Grand Prix, AM/FM/LW/SW signal seeking
Grand Prix, AM/FM signal seeking (US band)

1971

914-4

Blaupunkt
Wolfsburg, AM/LW
Wolfsburg - US, AM
Emden, AM/FM/LW
Emden - US, AM/FM

914-6

Blaupunkt
Boston, AM (US band)
Frankfurt, AM/FM/LW/SW
Frankfurt - US, AM/FM
Köln, AM/FM/LW signal seeking
New York, AM/FM/SW signal seeking (US band)

Becker
Grand Prix, AM/FM/LW/SW signal seeking
Grand Prix, AM/FM signal seeking (US band)

1970 914-6 not fitted with a radio

Dealer-installed VW Saphire radio

1972

Blaupunkt
Wolfsburg, AM/LW
Wolfsburg - US, AM
Emden, AM/FM/LW
Emden - US, AM/FM

1973-1974

Blaupunkt
Wolfsburg, AM/LW
Wolfsburg - US, AM
Emden, AM/FM/LW
Emden - US, AM/FM
Hannover, AM/FM/LW cassette

1975-1976

Blaupunkt
Braunschweig, AM/FM
Emden, AM/FM/LW
Emden - US, AM/FM

Turn signal switch 914-6

European spec. non-factory Blaupunkt radio with shorter FM band

Factory-installed Japanese-spec. radio with unusual FM band

Steering Column

The 914-6 upper steering column of 1970 and 1971 had a similar appearance to the 911s of the time. Most of its components were not shared directly, though. The plastic housing around the steering wheel hub consisted of upper and lower halves which held the wiper and turn signal switches.

The switch on the left, activated the turn signals when moved up or down and dimmed the headlights when moved fore and aft. On the right was the wiper/washer switch. Both of these switches looked like those on 911s and had the same rubber knobs and indicator decals. The 914-6 switches could not be interchanged with the 911 due to differences in the wiring.

The 260 1972 914-6s that were built (not sold in the US) used the 1972 four-cylinder's steering column and switches, as well as the two-speed wipers used on the 914-4. The steering column also had the ignition switch incorporated into the right-side housing.

The four-cylinder cars all had the ignition switch on the right side of the metal steering column housing. The 1970 and 1971 cars had only one column switch, the turn signal/headlight dimmer switch, which was on the left side of the column. The wiper/washer switch was dash-mounted. This black painted flat lever was more Volkswagen-like.

Turn signal switch early 914-4

Ignition switch 914-4 1970-1974

Wiper/washer switch 1970-71 914-6

Left and right column levers were used 1972-1976

In 1972, things changed. The turn signal/dimmer switch was still on the left side of the column, but the switch itself was a new design along with the column housing. On the right, in addition to the ignition switch, was a washer/wiper switch. The washer still operated on the spare tire power source, as before. An intermittent wiper option was available first in 1973. The stalk-type switch was identical to the standard washer/wiper except a fourth position was added. The switch on cars without this option had the same switch but a non-removeable tab made it impossible to move the lever to the interval position. The interval length was not variable. This switch arrangement was used through 1974.

For 1975-1976 the theme was the same for the column, but both switches were new. The housing changed from metal to a pot metal casting with a plastic cover. The ignition switch had been modified to VW Rabbit-type with a black crown around the protruding lock.

Ignition switch 1975-1976

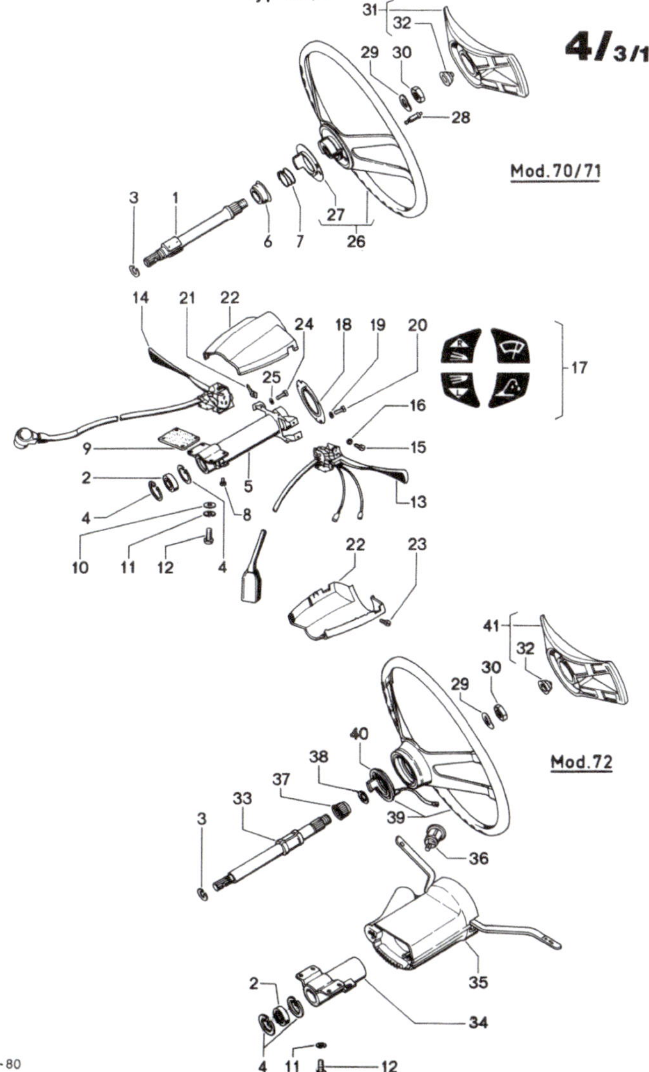

Illustration 4/3/1, 914-6

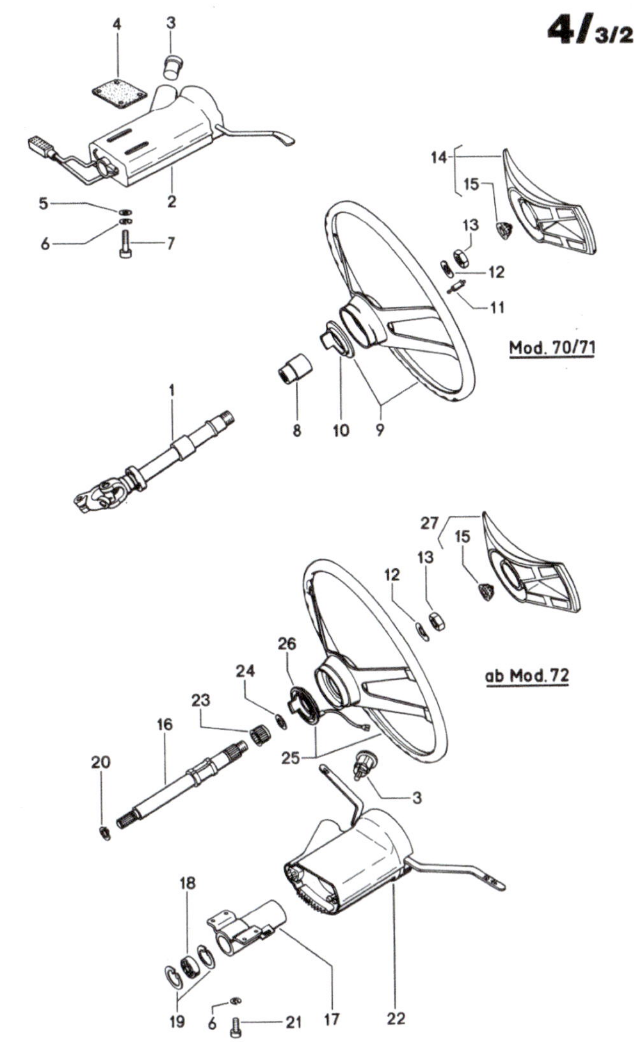

Illustration 4/3/2, 914-4

Leather-covered steering wheel came standard in several option packages

Standard hard rubber steering wheel

Steering Wheel

All 914-6s and US-specification four-cylinder cars used the same horn pads, with the Porsche crest embossed in the center; 914s for other countries had the Wolfsburg crest instead. The horn pad was modified at the 1972 model change to include a tab with wire attached (rather than the earlier 911-type horn contact stalk) which operated the horn. This later style proved troublesome, as the tab would break off, making the horn inoperable and no replacement part was available.

The four-spoke steering wheels on 914s had a family resemblance to contemporary 911s. The 380 mm diameter was smaller than the 400 mm ones used on 911s with the exception of the 1973 Carrera.

The 914-6 came standard with a hard rubber steering wheel rim encompassing four plastic-coated steel spokes. A leather-covered rim was optional. With the steering column change of 1972 came a new wheel for the final year of the 914-6. This wheel had leather covering and was shared with the 4-cylinder cars.

The steering wheels on four-cylinder cars were similar in appearance to the 914-6 wheels, but were not interchangeable, because the fours had an additional plastic hub attached. It is possible to remove this hub which then allows the wheel to be used on the six-cylinder car.

There were two steering wheel types fitted to four-cylinder cars for 1970 and 1971. One was hard rubber and the other was the optional leather-covered wheel. Steering wheels were modified for the 1972 model, since the steering column was changed and required a different steering wheel hub. Again there were hard rubber and leather-covered versions and they differed in the horn contact mounting from their predecessors. The hard rubber one continued to be offered through the end of production, but from the 1974 model year, the leather-covered wheel was replaced by one made from foamed imitation leather.

1974-1976 foamed imitation-leather steering wheel with pretend stitching

Wolfsburg crest horn button used on non-US market 914s

Early left visor with pocket

Left visor from 1976 with the final type of plastic pivots

Sun Visors, Mirror

Despite the fact that the early 914 sun visors had a 901 part number prefix, they were used only on the 914. The visor on the driver's side had a pocket for holding things. They were black vinyl on both sides and were modified only once for the 1972 model year. The new passenger's side visor featured a vanity mirror; although the driver's side remained much as before. At this time the mounting clips were also made taller. Early mounting pegs were metal. From 1974-on they were plastic.

At least one 916 had visors similar to those in similar period 911 coupes, black on the down side and white on the up side. Unlike 911s, they were actually perforated on the white side using the same material as the headliner. Other 916s had hand-sewn, leather-covered visors.

Prototype mirror with smaller base

Production version mirror used 1970-1971

Early right visor without vanity mirror

Right side visor with vanity mirror

The rear view mirror used on the 914 was the day/night type, secured to the windshield by the same adhesive pad used on the 911. There was one modification to the mirror at the beginning of the 1972 model year. The height of this mirror was greater than its predecessor (*see photos*).

Seats

Aside from the car's exterior styling, the most controversial area of the 1970-1971 914s was the seating arrangement. The driver had a conventional seat which could be set at several angles; reclining was hampered by the engine's location. The adjuster lever changed from straight to curved late in the 1970 model year. The passenger, however, received a fixed seat and a carpet-covered, tethered footrest.

The 1970 driver's seat was available in the materials and colors listed in the chart on page 122. Inserts were cloth, corduroy or basket-weave vinyl. The passenger's seatback was an integral part of the upholstery panel that covered the front of the firewall. It was covered with a smooth pebble grain vinyl. The insert area matched the driver's seat. The passenger's seat cushion resembled the lower part of the driver's seat, but was wider and bolted to the floor instead of being on adjustable rails.

In 1971 the choice of material for the seats was different, but the configuration was unchanged. Though basket-weave seat inserts were listed by the factory for 1971, it appears a change to smooth leather-grained Naugahyde vinyl occurred before November 1970.

This larger mirror was fitted from 1972-1976

Seating arrangement with early vinyl and basket weave upholstery

Black/white/tan hound's tooth seat inserts used in 1970 and early 1971

1972-1973 cars had many changes, but the most the significant for occasional occupants was the new movable passenger seat and the disappearance of the footrest. The vinyl used on bolsters and the rear upholstery panel was also a new smooth grain, although essentially the same colors were offered.

In 1974 the seat rails were changed on both seats preventing them from being adjusted as far forward as was possible with the earlier type. For US

Corduroy seat inserts 1970 914-6

Smooth grained Naugahyde vinyl used for most of 1971

Adjustable right seat was introduced in 1972

Tartan seat inserts were new in 1975

The short-lived seat belt interlock system

Standard upholstery 1976. Note retractable seat belts

One of the 914-6 GT seating configurations

buyers there was an electrical pick-up for the seat belt warning system which set off a buzzer reminding them to buckle up. Materials were unchanged from 1972, but by February 1974 some cars had the pleats in the seats formed by heat pressing, rather than being sewn, as the earlier seats had been.

Bold new materials ushered in 1975, such as the tartan cloth seat inserts, which could be ordered to brighten up the interior. The vinyl also changed, as did the pattern of the basket-weave vinyl (same as VW Rabbit) and wider ribs on corduroy. US cars again had the seat belt buzzer wiring, now with an interlock feature preventing the car from being started if the driver's seat belt was not buckled. The interlock feature was first used in August 1973 and continued through December 1974. These were all subsequently disabled. No additional changes were made.

The seat belts that were used from 1970 through the end of 1971 were adjustable but non-retracting. The later-style retractable belts that appeared January 1,1972 were vastly superior and gave the interior a neater appearance. An optional third seat belt was provided for occupants riding between the seats on the *third seat*.

Seat belts used in 1970-1971

Retractable seat belt buckle

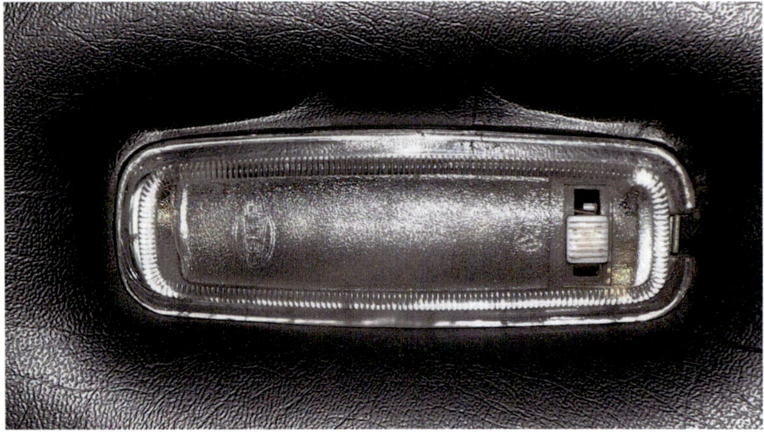
Interior light used in all 914s

Between the seats in the middle of the upholstery panel was an interior light with chrome-colored rim which lit when the doors were opened or when it was manually switched on. This light was a standard Volkswagen part and remained unchanged throughout the seven-year production run.

Center Console

Between the driver's and passenger's footwells was an upholstered partition referred to as a deposit in the parts manuals. These were carpeted to match either felt or loop floor carpet in 1970 and 1971. They were modified in 1972 and then again in 1975. The 916 had one that held a solitary fuel gauge at the top.

Center deposit on the 914-6

1972 916 featured a upmarket console with fuel gauge

The optional console was offered from 1973

Center console with angled gauges with dealer-installed DPD air-conditioning

Center console with staggered gauges with dealer-installed VPC air-conditioning

914-6 models had a hand throttle in front of the shift lever

A center console housing the three instruments (described on page 67) was standard on the 1973 2.0 models. It extended back from the dashboard surrounding both the shift lever and the heater control lever and was made of black vinyl-covered fiberboard. It was optional on 1974-1976 models. The console was modified when dealer-installed air conditioning was fitted (*see photos on page 70*).

Four-cylinder cars had only the heat lever behind the shift lever

Shift Mechanism

The shift levers were interchangeable between 1970-1972 four and all six-cylinder cars. The knob, boot and much of the mechanism below the shift lever were from the 911, although the lever was exclusively 914. A Sportomatic shift lever (and appropriate pedal assembly) is illustrated in the parts manual and was rarely fitted (*see pages 109-110 for additional information*).

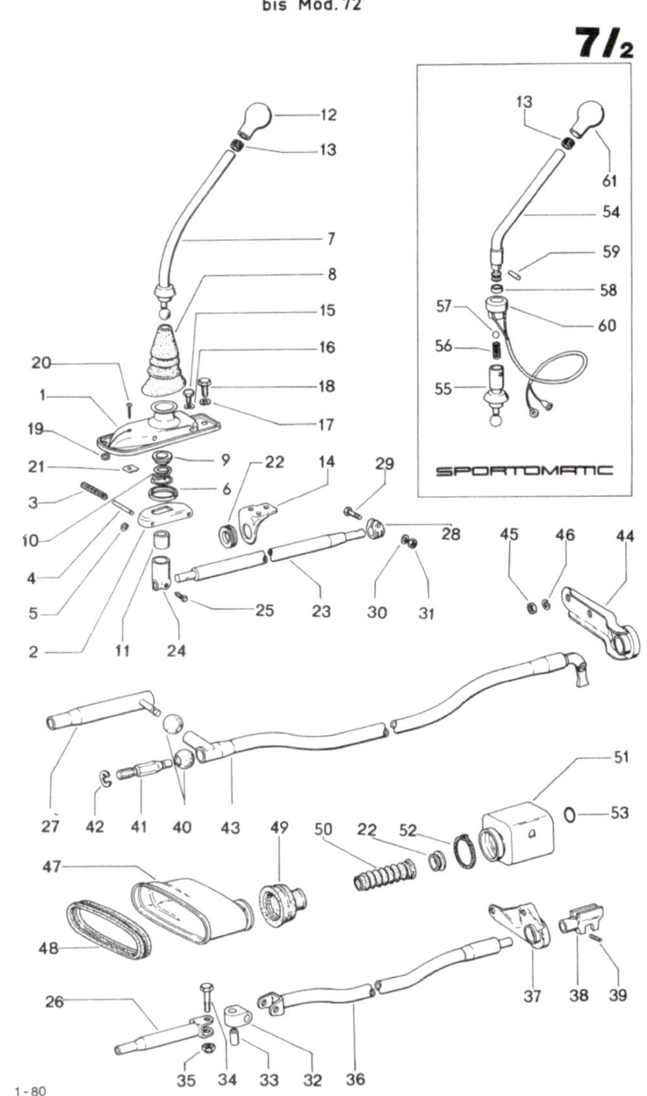

Illustraion 7/2 — rear shift linkage

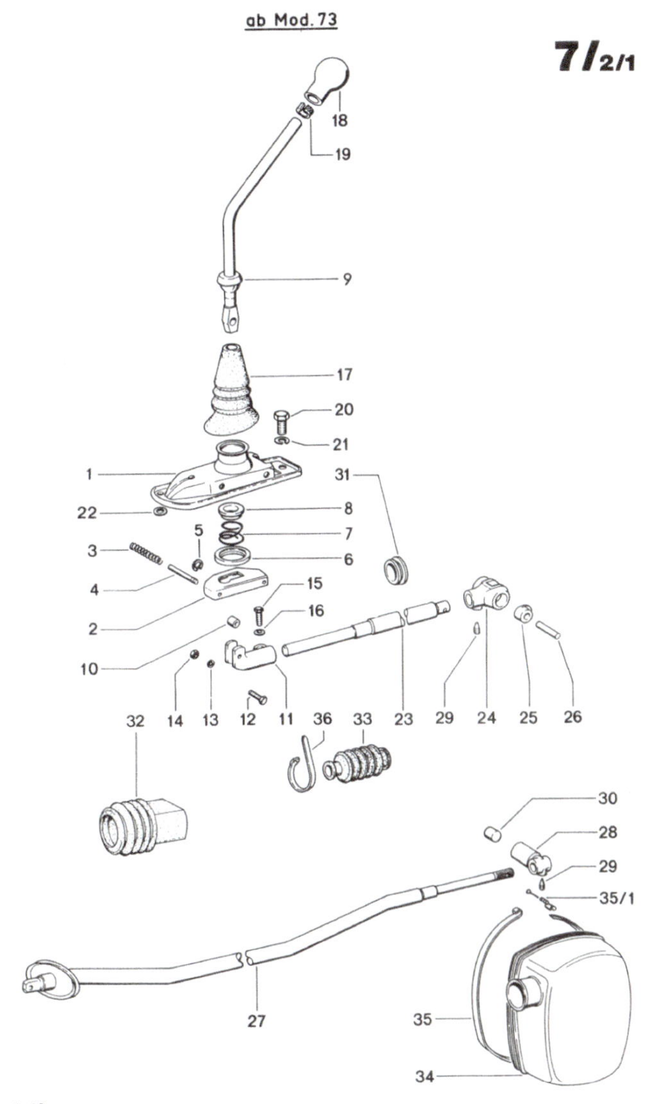

Illustration 7/2/1 — side shift linkage

When optional center console was fitted 1973-1976, a leather shift boot was installed and the heater lever was altered

914-6 GT tunnel dispensed with the heat lever, kept the hand throttle and added an electrical kill switch behind the shifter

The shift knob used on the majority of 914s, left. Rare Sportomatic, right

1972 heater knob

Defrost light added in 1973

The shift linkage was radically altered in 1973, quieting much of the criticism about vagueness which surrounded the earlier design. About the only parts retained were the shift knob and boot. On cars with the appearance group, a leather boot covered the lower third of the shift lever.

Other Floor Mounted Controls

The hand throttle on the 914-6 was mounted on the center tunnel on the shifter base in front of the shift lever, although this location was somewhat less than ideal from an ergonomic standpoint. Its black cylindrical knob was the same one used on contemporary 911s.

Center tray with divider

The heat control lever used a red knob similar in shape to the hand throttle knob. It was located behind the shift lever. Pulling up on the lever opened doors in the two valves underneath the car which directed the heated air from the heat exchangers. With the lever up the heated air was directed into the passenger's compartment. Pulling it farther back activated an electric fan in the engine compartment to force heated air to flow at an increased rate.

In 1972 US specification cars received a new knob, as used on the 911. It had the words DEFROST, ON and OFF with helpful arrows to direct use. In 1973 US spec. cars, which reverted to the early plain red knob, but a lighted defroster ON/OFF warning light was added to the floor in front of the lever. 1973-1976 914s fitted with consoles had a different shaped chrome-plated lever with a round red screw-on knob.

Between the seats at floor level was a molded urethane tray in which an optional upholstered block of foam could be installed. So that the 914 could be classified as having three-person carrying capacity, this was euphemistically referred to as a *seat*. The third seat was upholstered to match the seat bolsters. The tray was modified in 1971 so that it consisted of two compartments instead of one.

Early center tray without divider

Center "seat" early 914

Storage box in later cars with optional console. Note location of defrost light

In 1973 a vinyl-covered wooden storage box with hinged lid was offered on 2.0 models and as an option on all 1974 and later cars (when the optional center console with instruments was fitted). The lid was upholstered to match the seat upholstery fitting in the same location as the third seat.

The frame in front of the seats and along the side of the center tunnel by the sides of the seats was covered with vinyl which matched the seat bolsters on 1970-1974 models. For 1975-1976 these areas were just painted flat black.

Normal pedal configuration

Unique center seat area of the 916

Storage space was decidedly minimal

Pedals, Handbrake

The pedals in all 914s were the same as those in contemporary 911s. The pads on the brake and clutch, in fact, were initially used in 1954. The entire sub-assembly beneath the floor was totally 911, and the accelerator was standard 911, as well. Even the bracket and stop bolt for the accelerator were shared. This bracket was attached to the wooden floorboard that covered the lower pedal assembly.

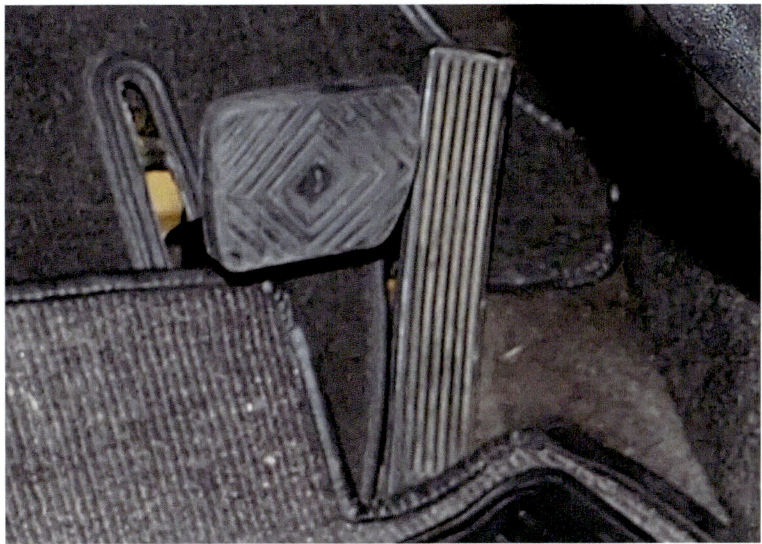

Pedal configuration with Sportomatic gearbox

Early handbrake in off position with rubber boot. Lever at rear adjusts seat angle

The handbrake lever was on the left side of the driver's seat. Had the lever remained raised when engaged, entry and exit would have been difficult for the driver, so the top of the lever was designed to drop back to the disengaged position after the driver set the brake. To disengage the parking brake the driver had to pull up the lever, push the button and hold it in and then let the lever back down. This no doubt caused confusion, as well as frequent brake replacement.

In 1973 the earlier unit was replaced with a one-piece angled unit, mounted lower, which operated in the conventional manner. It was necessary to retool the inner longitudinal panel because there was not sufficient clearance to lower this revised handbrake lever; and gone was the rubber boot and handbrake lever stop welded on the early cars.

Some later GT models had the handbrake relocated to the area between the seats for competition use in rallies.

Later handbrake which operated in a normal fashion

Door-Related Items

The door panels on 914s were fairly austere. The driver's side featured an armrest with a hinging top forming a lid to the narrow storage compartment below. The hard rubber top was always black, but the compartment below was color-coordinated with the door panel until late 1974 when they all became black as well. The passenger did not have a compartment on his side, but got something better, a grab handle. The handle and top of the passenger's arm rest were black with the lower support piece matching the door panel.

Changes in door panels corresponded with changes in upholstery materials occurring at 1971, 1972 and 1975. The panels used in 1970 were a smooth pebble-grained vinyl and in 1971 were smooth leather-grained Naugahyde vinyl. The 1972 through 1974 cars had brick pattern that matched the 1970-1974 dashboard insert. In 1975, this changed to a somewhat different

Very early 1971 smooth pebble-grain vinyl door panel and storage compartment

1973 door panel from 914-4 with basket-weave seat inserts

1971 door panel from 914-4 with smooth Naugahyde seat inserts

Door panel 1974

Door panel 1976 with late-style brick pattern vinyl

Door panel 916 (Porsche cloth was not originally fitted)

basket-weave pattern. Two additional changes were noted, one in January 1972 at chassis number 472 290 9017 when the panel structure went from two-piece steel and flat wood chip board to a one-piece molded cardboard panel. A change also occurred at the 1973 model year when the door was structurally modified.

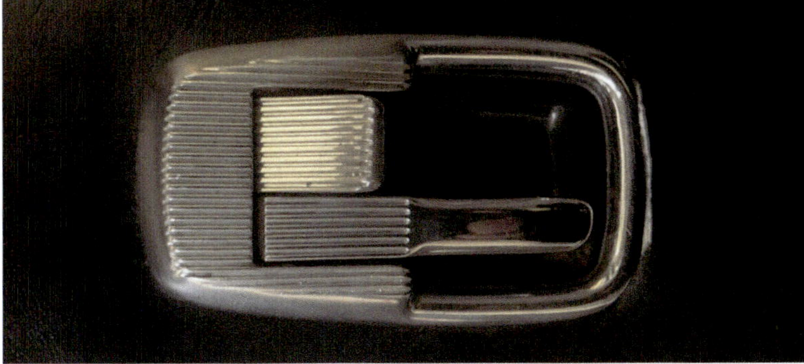
Early inside door handle

Inner door handle used from February/March 1970-1972

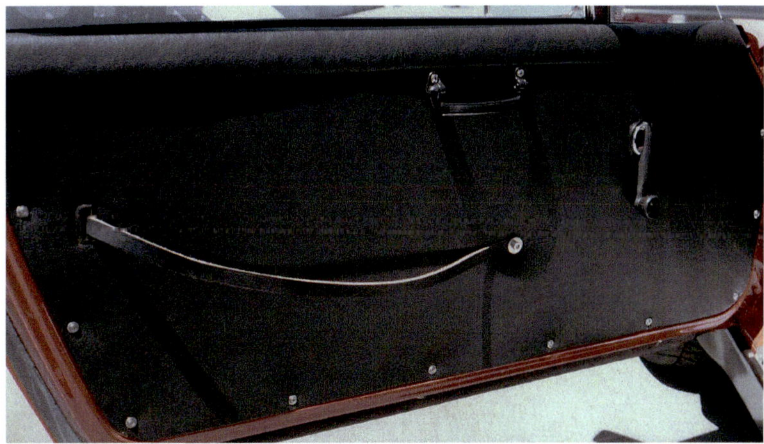
GT door panel with leather strap door release, grab handle and window crank

916 passenger's door panel

The 914-6 GT had a lightweight, flat door panel with a simple leather door pull. The normal window lift mechanism was still fitted, though.

The 916 door panel had an elastic map pocket on the driver's side. The passenger's side equipment was similar to the standard 914, except for the door pull upper center. The pleated pattern and leather material gave the 916 a much more upmarket appearance.

The inside door handle was another part used on period Volkswagens. It incorporated a locking mechanism and the early style was chrome-plated. There was a running change in February/March 1970, although there was no change in part number. The handle part was slightly larger in diameter on the later cars (*see photos*). When the door changed in late 1973, so did the housing for the inside handle. It now had a one-piece black plastic covering.

Window cranks were also standard Volkswagen items. Those used in 1970 through June/July 1973 had chrome at the base and a plastic-covered handle. In June/July 1973 the handle was replaced by one that looked about the

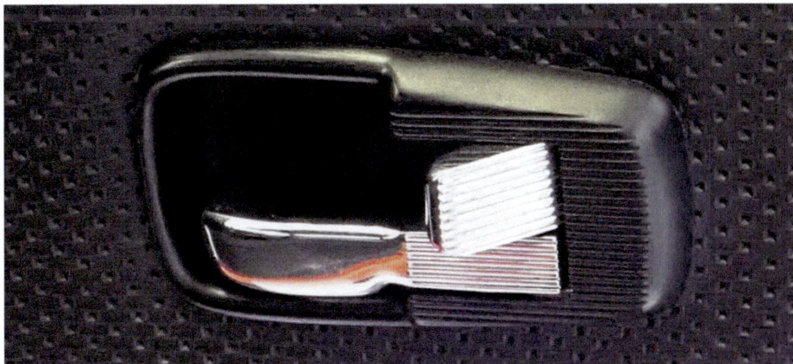
1973-1976 door handle with black plastic surround

Window crank through mid-1973

Mid-1973-1974 window crank

Window crank 1975-1976

1973 door stay & interior light switch

same but was totally covered by black plastic. The cranks used in 1975 and 1976 were the fat plastic ones used on contemporary Volkswagen Rabbits.

Fastened to the perimeter of the door was a foam seal (*illustration 8/6, number 34*), one of two seals for the door. The other (*number 35*) mounted to the threshold and covered the seam where outer and inner body panels came together. Neither seal was modified throughout production.

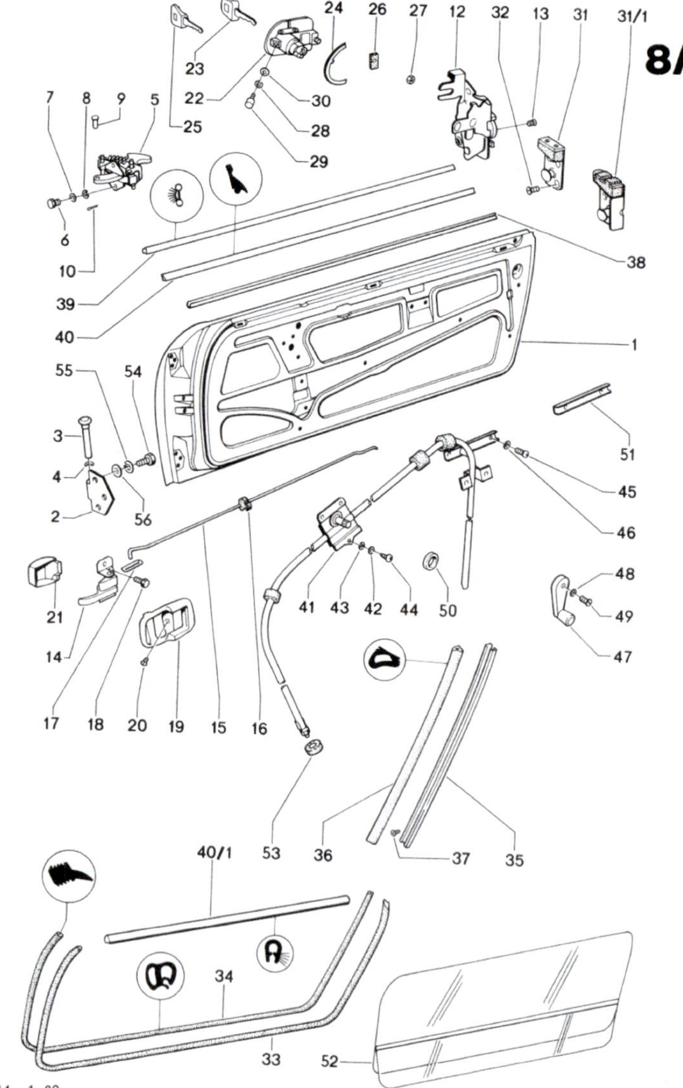

Illustration 8/6

Threshold

Starting up front at the hinge post, one encountered the hinges, door stay and interior light switch. The first two never changed, but the interior light switch had four incarnations. US cars had multiple pole switches with both hot and ground wires, due to the ignition buzzer. Non-US cars had fewer wires since the switches only operated the interior light. A change was made in 1973 to eliminate the hot wire, although the part was not substantially modified. There were again US and RoW (*Rest of World*) versions. All four varieties had Volkswagen origins.

A Karmann coachbuilder plate was also located on the hinge post. It was stamped with both the chassis number and paint number on four-cylinder cars. On the 914-6, only the paint number was stamped. An additional paint sticker was located on the hinge post inside the driver's door on 1976 models.

The 914-6 paint plate (left) did not include the Karmann number

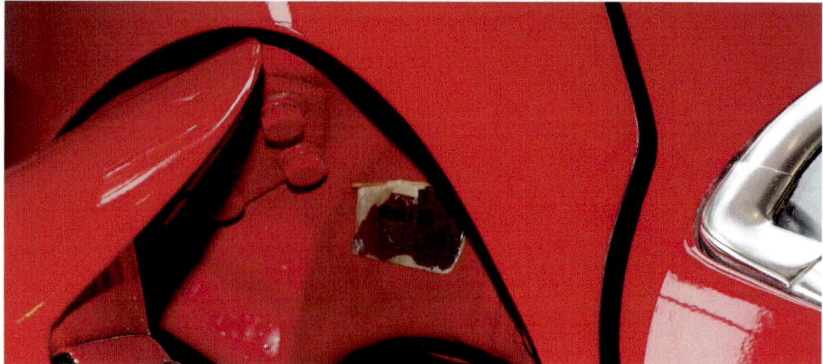

Paint sticker was located inside the driver's door

Early aluminum threshold rails with white plastic rivets

Late plastic threshold rails with black plastic rivets

The bottom of the threshold had two extruded plates. The outer one was wider and secured by white plastic rivets. The plates were originally made from aluminum and had a ribbed upper surface. In March 1973 at chassis number 473 291 8919, the material was changed to black plastic. The plastic mounting rivets were changed from white to black at this time.

The inner rail covered the body seam and carpet edge. It followed the same material progression in 1973. This rail was secured with Phillips-head screws.

The air exhaust vents and striker plates of the rear threshold (lock post), are described on page 35. US-spec. cars had a sticker on the left lock post stating the car's conformity to DOT and EPA regulations. This included the month and year of manufacture and the chassis number. From January 1972 the gross weight vehicle rating, as well as the front and rear axle gross weight ratings were added initially at the bottom, moving up in 1975.

914-6 silver only, maufacturer is Dr. Ing. h.c. F. Porsche KG

914-4 silver or black depending on exterior color. There are five types and maufacturer is Volkswagenwerk AG:

1) Through 12/71
2) 1/72 through 8/72 (end of 1972 model year), vehicle and axle weights added at bottom left, TYPE PASSENGER CAR at bottom right
3) 9/72 through 1/75, TYPE PASSENGER CAR at top left
4) 1/75, TYPE PASSENGER CAR at bottom left, weights are moved up
5) 2/75 on, Germany added after Volkswagenwerk AG

Door jamb 1974 2.0 from Japan

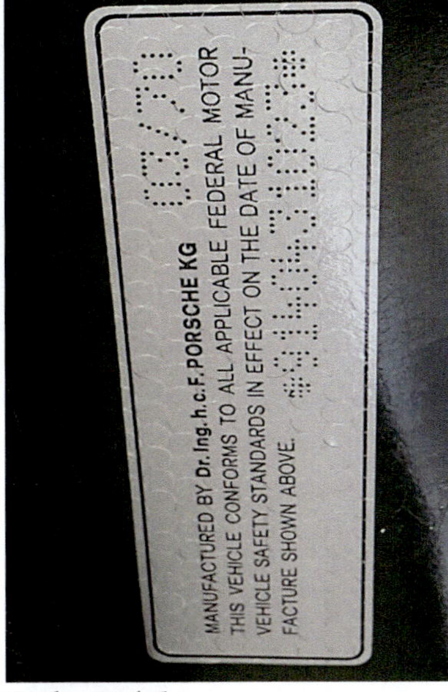

Sticker 914-6

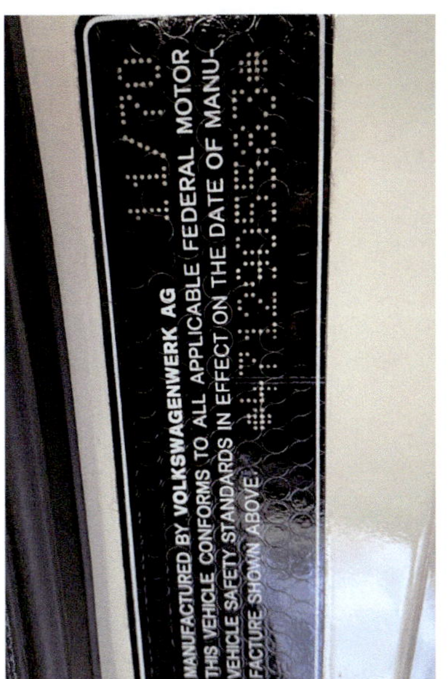

First type 914-4 sticker, black

First type 914-4 sticker, silver

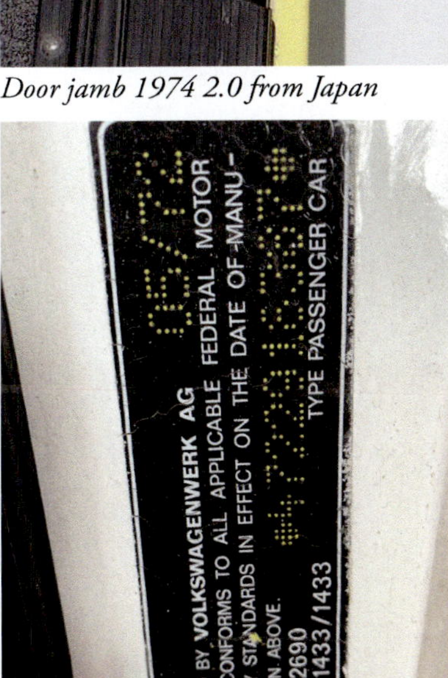

Second type sticker, car was repainted

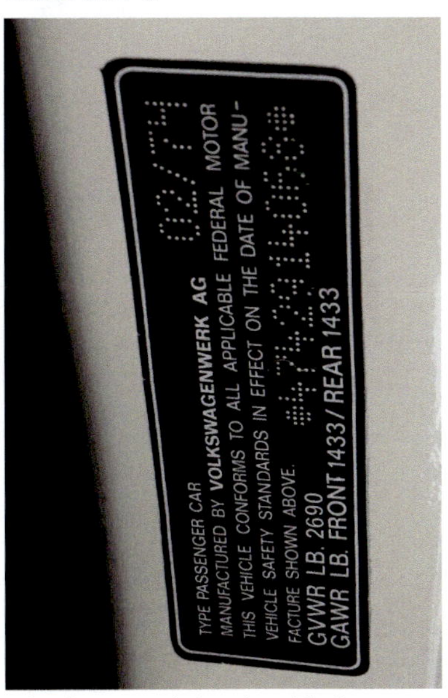

Third type 914-4 sticker, black

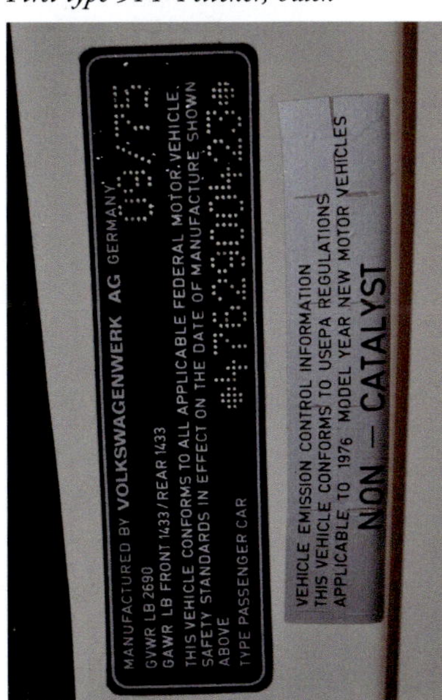

Final type sticker, not California spec.

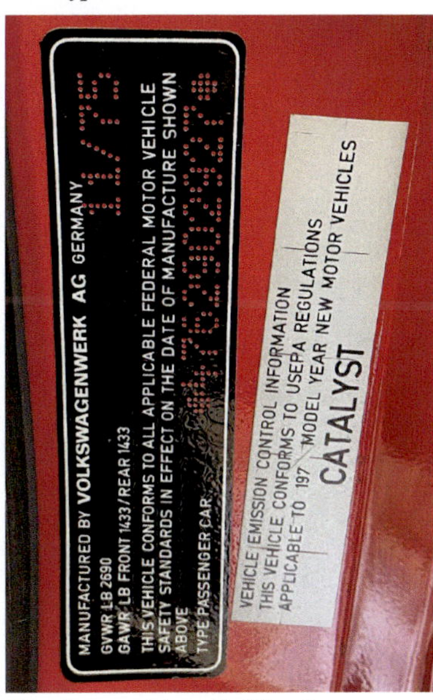

Final type sticker, California spec.

Felt carpet, 1970 914-6

Loop carpet, 1976 2.0

Footwell was deeper 1970-1971

Footwell was shortened in 1972 when the footrest was removed

Carpeting

Carpeting covered the floor area and threshold area in all 914s. Front luggage compartment carpet is described on page 58, and rear luggage carpet is described on page 61.

Standard carpeting material in 914-4s was felt, but optional loop carpet was available for all years and models. Loop carpeting was standard on all US specification cars from 1974 through 1976. The 914-6 had felt carpet in 1970 and loop in 1971-1972 models. The color listing on pages 122 and 123 shows the colors available and their corresponding codes. Modifications in carpeting followed the equipment fitted, model differences and material changes. The 916 used 911 velour carpeting.

Footrest was color coordinated with the carpet

The passenger's wooden footrest that was standard in 1970 and 1971 was totally covered by carpet, matching the type used in the rest of the interior. When it disappeared in January 1972, a larger foam filler was installed under the carpet to shorten the footwell. This significant change occurred at the same time when retractable seat belts were added.

Coat Hook

Coat hooks were mounted on the side upholstery above the driver's shoulder. Starting in 1971, the passenger received one also. The black plastic coat hooks were the same as used on contemporary 911s. The location on the inner roof pillar above the seats did not afford a great deal of room for hanging coats.

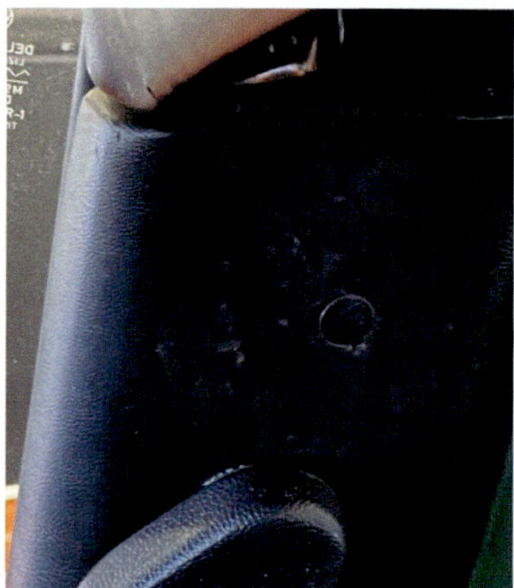
Coat hooks were on both sides except in 1970 when a plug was on the right

Engine Compartment

Engine Types

The chart below describes the engine options available for each of the seven years that 914s were produced. Following this is a brief year by year description of mechanical specifications and then more detailed descriptions of externally visible components.

914-4

Displacement	Horse-power	Engine Type	Engine Code	Starting Number
1970				
1.7 liter	80 hp	022	W	W 0 000 001
1971				
1.7 liter	80 hp	022	W	W 0 057 461
1972				
1.7 liter	80 hp	022	W	W 0 129 582
1.7 liter	80 hp	022	EA	EA 0 000 001 USA
1973				
1.7 liter	80 hp	022	W	W 0 170 001 Europe
1.7 liter	80 hp	022	EA	EA 0 057 001 USA
1.7 liter	72 hp	022	EB	EB 0 000 001 California
2.0 liter	95 hp	039	GA	GA 0 000 001 USA
2.0 liter	100 hp	039	GB	GB 0 000 001 Europe
1974				
1.8 liter	76 hp	022	EC	EC 0 000 001 USA
1.8 liter (V)	85 hp	021	AN	AN 0 000 001 Europe
2.0 liter	95 hp	039	GA	GA 0 006 766 USA
2.0 liter	100 hp	039	GB	GB 0 007 402 Europe
1975				
1.8 liter	76 hp	022	EC	EC 0 037 552 USA
1.8 liter (V)	85 hp	021	AN	AN 0 008 798 Europe
2.0 liter	100 hp	039	GB	GB 0 009 822 Europe
2.0 liter	88 hp	039	GC	GC 0 000 001 USA
1976				
1.8 liter	76 hp	022	EC	EC 0 045 073 USA
1.8 liter (V)	85 hp	021	AN	AN 0 008 899 Europe
2.0 liter	100 hp	039	GB	GB 0 010 779 Europe
2.0 liter	88 hp	039	GC	GC 0 002 915 USA

914-6

Displacement	Horse-power	Engine Type	Trans. Type	Starting Number
1970				
2.0 liter	110 hp	901/36	5-spd	640 0001 Europe
2.0 liter	110 hp	901/37	Sporto	640 3001 Europe
2.0 liter	110 hp	901/38	5-spd	640 4001 USA
2.0 liter	110 hp	901/39	Sporto	640 7001 USA
1971				
2.0 liter	110 hp	901/36	5-spd	641 0001 Europe
2.0 liter	110 hp	901/37	Sporto	641 3001 Europe
2.0 liter	110 hp	901/38	5-spd	641 4001 USA
2.0 liter	110 hp	901/39	Sporto	641 7001 USA
1972				
2.0 liter	110 hp	901/36	5-spd	642 0001 Europe

914-6 GT

Displacement	Horse-power	Engine Type	Trans. Type
1970-1972			
2.0 liter	220 hp	901/25	5-spd

916

Displacement	Horse-power	Engine Type	Trans. Type
1972			
2.4 liter	190 hp	911/56	5-spd
2.6 liter	210 hp	911/86	5-spd

1970

The 914-4 022 W (Wolfsburg) 1679 cc engine was derived from the new generation Volkswagen 411 engine. This power plant featured a magnesium case and forged crankshaft with four main bearings. With a compression ratio of 8.2:1, 80 horsepower was produced at 4900 rpm. Bosch D-Jetronic fuel injection was developed in conjunction with Volkswagen under patent rights provided by Bendix of America. An electric fuel pump provided a constant flow to the injectors and returned excess fuel back to the tank. The flexibility of this system allowed it to be used for all world markets as emission standards continued to evolve.

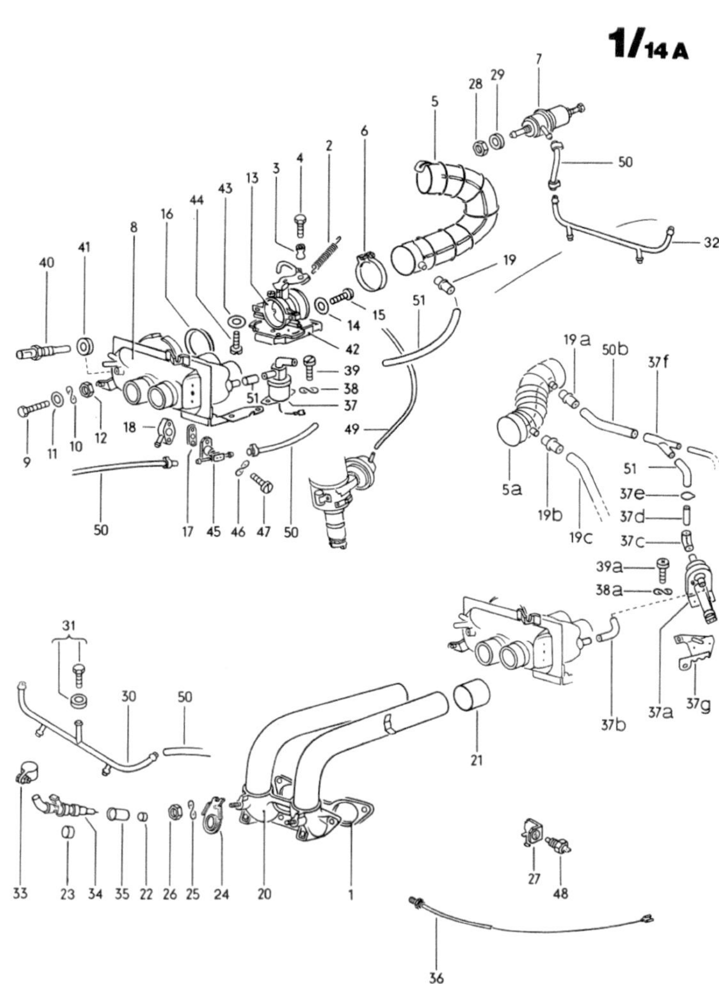

Illustration 1/14 A, Bosch D-Jetronic Fuel injection components

The four-cylinder engine was located as far away from the interior area as possible to minimize noise and had a bar at the front that served as a mount. It had two rubber mounts at the outer chassis mount points.

The 914-6 engine weighed over 100 lbs. more than the four-cylinder equivalent. It was effectively the 1991 cc 911T engine used in 1969. The 1970 version of 911 engines had been enlarged to 2.2 liter, giving the 911 a foot up to the new lower-priced 914. The six-cylinder engine featured 8.6:1 compression, CD ignition and 40 mm Weber 40 IDT P 1 3 C carburetors.

Engine numbers were initially located on the fan support, which was where they were located on 911s. Very shortly into production they were moved to the top of the engine case.

The oil reservoir for the dry sump system was located on the left side of the engine, as opposed to the right side on the contemporary 911. The small rear lid grille was located in a less than desirable air-flow position and despite the lack of the drain tray on the four-cylinder cars, this caused the engine to run around 10° F hotter than in the 911.

The first 914-6 GT engines were designated 901/25 and were the same 1991 cc as the 914-6 to allow participation in racing classes limited to two liters. Horsepower output of 220 was achieved via the use of domed pistons, which resulted in 10.3:1 compression. Carburetors were modified Weber units from the 914-6.

1971

On four-cylinder cars baffles were added to the sump for better oil pickup during cornering.

1972

The 022 EA designation was given to US spec. engines. This engine could be run on regular grade gasoline due to minor changes in the fuel injection system and a different distributor advance configuration. Euro engines maintained the W engine code.

The 914-6 was discontinued at the end of the 1972 model year after a total of 3,360 examples were produced.

Eleven 916 models were produced during the 1972 model year. Engines designated 911/56 were essentially the 2341 cc 911S engine (911/53) used in 1972 models producing 190 hp. This engine featured Bosch mechanical fuel injection and high-voltage capacitor ignition as used on contemporary 911s. Larger displacement engines were later fitted to some cars.

1973

The 1.7 liter 022 EA was maintained for 49-state US cars, while California received 022 EB. The latter featured lower compression resulting in a drop to 72 hp. Euro spec. cars continued to use the 022 W engine.

New for 73 was a larger 1971 cc alternative developed by Porsche. Dubbed the 2.0 in most places (in the UK it was called the SC), it featured increased bore (94 mm) and stroke (71 mm). The 50-state US spec. 039 GA engine had dished pistons (7.6:1 compression ratio) and developed 95 hp, while Euro spec. 039 GB engines featured flat pistons (8:1 compression ratio) resulting in 100 hp. All of the 039 engines also had large valves and continued to use Bosch D-Jetronic fuel injection.

The engine support was modified in 1973 from pressed steel to cast iron. The dual flexible mounts were relocated from the outer part of the support to just below the engine.

1974

For 1974 the smaller 022 EC once again was approved for all US spec. applications. It featured larger valves and an increase in bore, from 90 mm to 93 mm, though the stroke remained the same. The resulting displacement of 1795 cc, referred to as the 1.8, produced 76 hp and was the first to utilize the new Bosch L-Jetronic fuel injection. In this form of fuel injection, referred to as AFC, fuel flow through the injectors was regulated by the air flow entering the combustion chambers.

A new 021 AN engine for the European market features twin one-barrel Solex 40 PDSIT carburetors. These are designated with *(V)* on page 87. Dimensions and valves mimicked the 1.8 above with higher compression, the AN engine produced 85 hp.

The 039 GA and 039 GB 2.0 engines were unaltered from the ones used in 1973.

1975

The 022 EC, 021 AN and 039 GB were unaltered from 1974. The 2.0 US version was referred to as the 039 GC and suffered horsepower loss to just 88. The losses were due to addition of air pumps to all and exhaust gas recirculation and catalytic converters on California-bound cars due to ever more stringent emission controls.

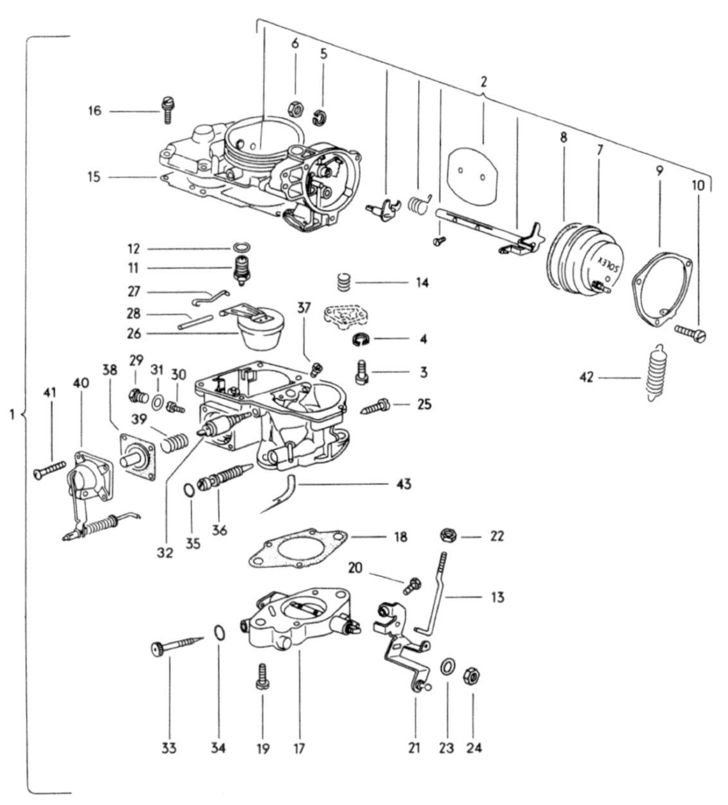

Illustration 1/12/2A, Solex 40 PDSIT carburetor

1/14/2 A

914 1-80

Illustration 1/14/2A, showing air-pump system used on US spec. cars

1976

All engines were unmodified from 1975. The US spec. 1.8 was discontinued prior to January of 1976.

914-4 production ended with 115,596 examples produced – 118,976 of all models.

Air Filters

914-4

The first 1.7 914-4 engines had steel oil bath air filters with no replaceable element. There were two versions used simultaneously in 1970-1971. The 1972 version was modified but was similar to the previous one and used a different inlet elbow. The one for California cars had an activated charcoal chamber.

The 1973 1.7 had a round plastic air filter housing with a round replaceable element. It did not have a pre-heat provision like on the earlier air filter.

Air filter 1970-1972

The 1.8 air cleaners were square and plastic and were mounted by a steel stand bolted to the left engine shelf. They used a new square paper element.

The air filter setup for the twin Solex PDSIT carburetors used on the

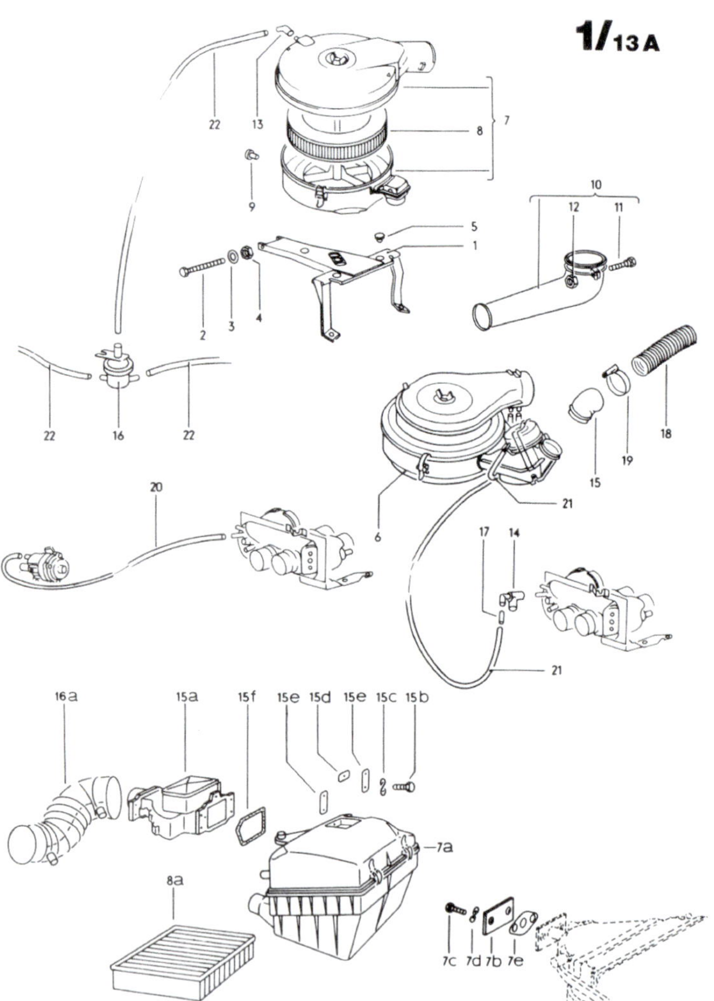

Illustration 1/13A, 914-4 air filters 1973 top, 1970-1972, middle, 1974-1976 1.8 bottom. 2.0 not illustrated

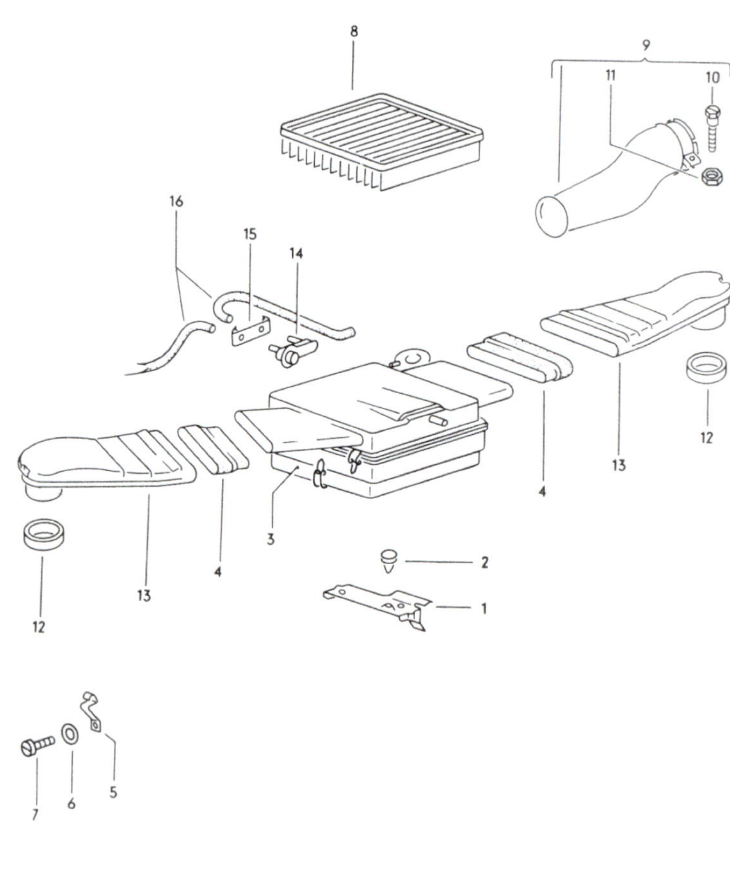

Illustration 1/12/3A, 914-4 air filter 1.8 Euro spec. fitted with carburetors

Air filter 1973 1.7

Air filter, 1975 2.0

021 AN Euro spec. engine was unlike any of the other configurations. It used a unique rectangular replaceable element.

The air filters on the 2.0 engines were much different than the smaller displacement engine setups, but used the same square paper element as the 1.8. US and European versions were the same. The early 1973 2.0 air filter had a cross hatch pattern. Late 1973-1974 models had ribbing. 1975-1976 had a larger outlet for the oil breather and a rectangular tube receiver for California emissions. Euro spec. 2.0 cars in 1975-1976 continued to use the earlier version.

1974 and later 1.8 air filter set up

Early 1973 2.0 air filter cover

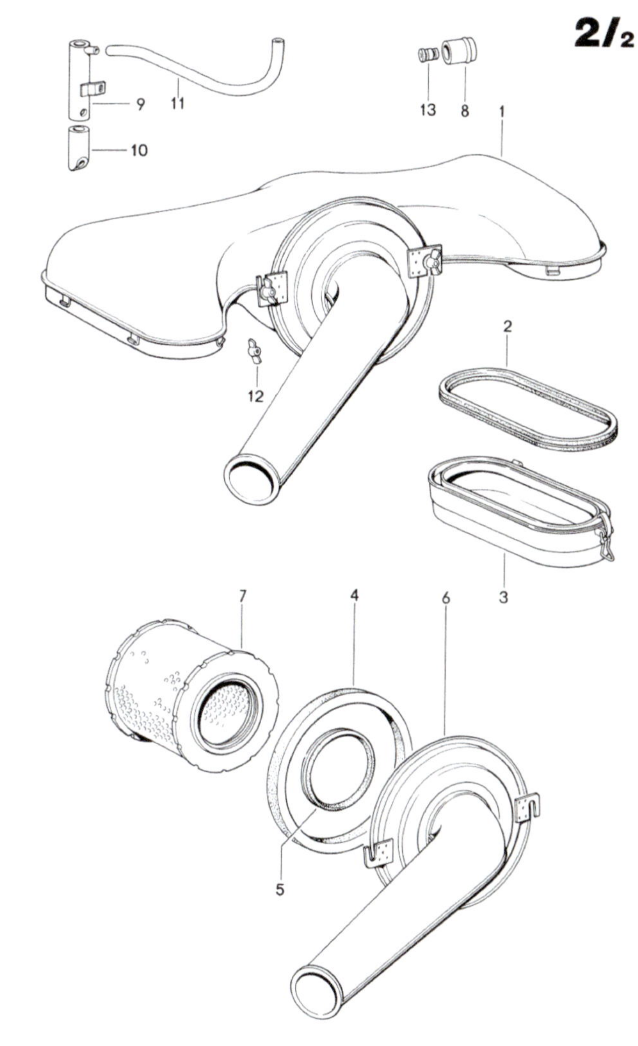

Illustration 2/2, 914-6 air filter

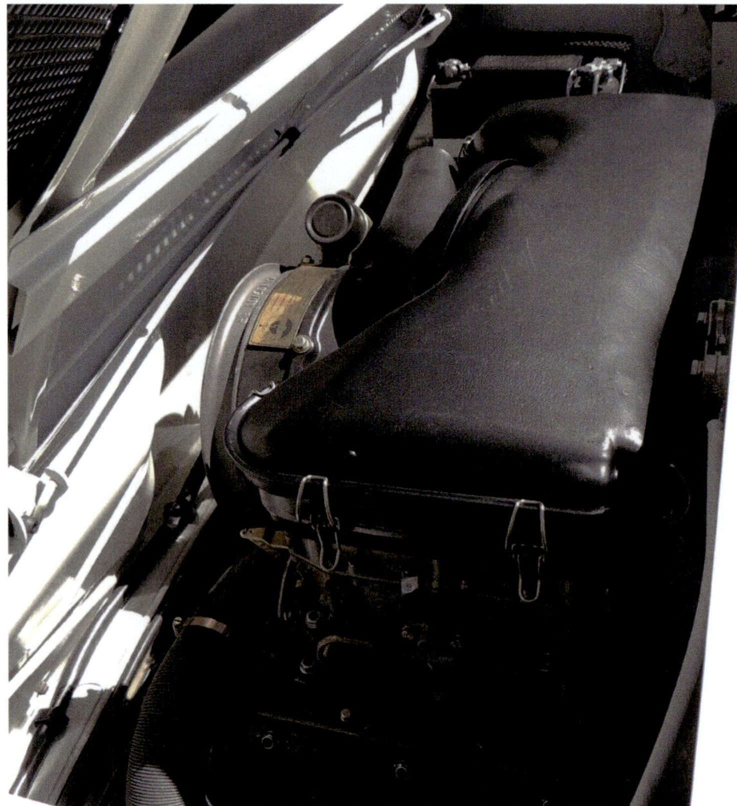

Air filter housing, 1970 914-6

1970 914-6 with air filter cover removed

914-6

The 914-6 air filter housing had a distinct family resemblance to its 911 counterpart, though it faced the opposite direction. It was made from plastic and was a bit stubbier since it needed to clear the rear grille. It used the same air filter as the period 911.

Fuel Pump

The four-cylinder injected cars had two different pumps. From 1970-1974 the 311.906.091 D (Bosch #0 580 463 005) pump was used. The pump was mounted under the battery shelf in the engine compartment above the heater control valve and hose. As a result these models were prone to vapor lock.

Shell decal on 1971 914-6. Note also decal on coil

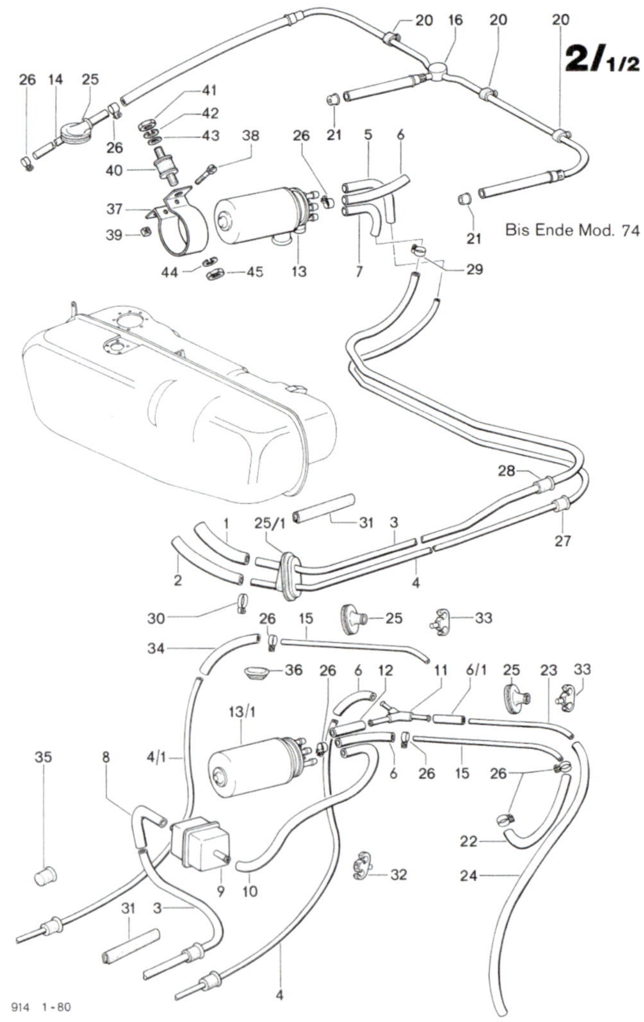

Illustration 2/1/2, rear-mounted 914-6 fuel pump top, 914-4 pump bottom

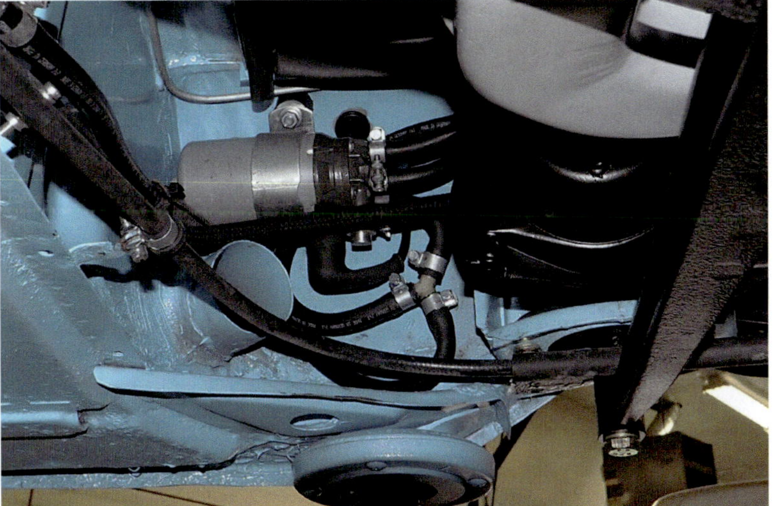

Rear-mounted fuel pump, 1973 914-4

The pump from 1975-1976 was 043.906.091 (Bosch# 0 580 463 016). It was relocated to the front compartment by the fuel tank which alleviated the vapor lock issue.

The carbureted 1.8 liter European cars had mechanical pumps. They mounted to the front of the engine on the lower left (driver's) side. The carbureted 914-6 had a low-pressure electric fuel pump shared with contemporary 911Ts in the same location as the 914-4. The Porsche number was 911.608.107.00 (Bosch #0 580 960 009).

Ab Mod. 75

2/1/3

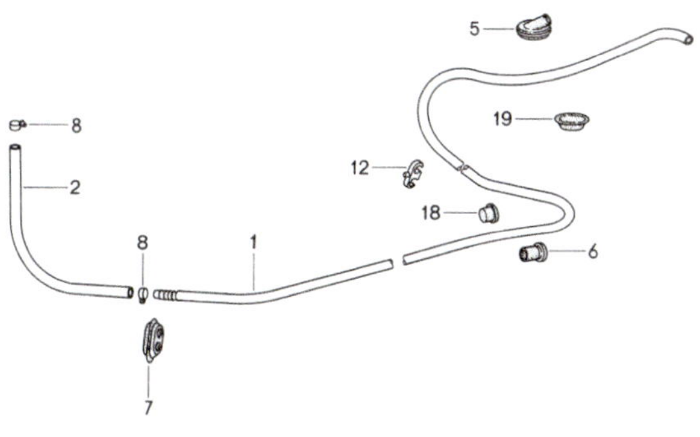

914 1-80

Illustration 2/1/3, front-mounted fuel pump 1975-1976

From 1975 the fuel pump was behind this cover in the front luggage area

Electrical Components

Relay/Circuit Board

On both engine types a unified-mounting plastic relay/circuit board, which incorporated multiple relays and was coated on the bottom with a tar-like substance, was located on the left side of the engine compartment wall. The basic subframe was different for four and six-cylinder cars and was not modified. The plastic cover was the same

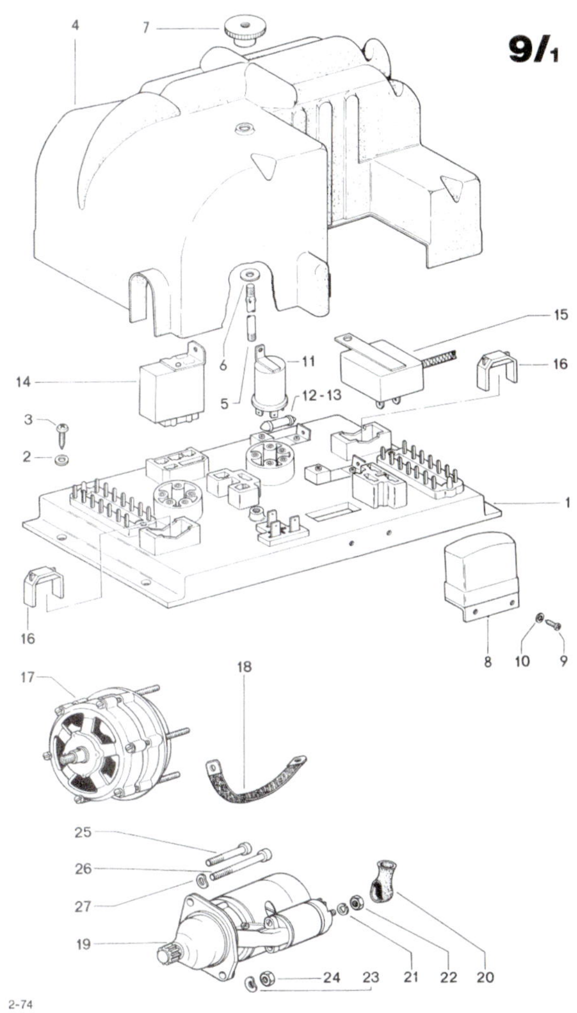

Illustration 9/1, relay/circuit board, voltage regulator, alternator & starter 914-4

1970-1971 circuit board cover. Note exposed voltage regulator

1975-1976 circuit board cover missing its rubber band

for all 1970-1971 models. This cover was secured by a steel stud with a knurled nut.

The relay/circuit board cover was modified in 1972 to clear the new retractable seatbelt recess in the firewall. For 1975 the nut and stud arrangement on the plastic relay/circuit board cover, which frequently caused damage that led to water leaks, was replaced with a round rubber band.

Uncovered unit on 914-6 GT. Note also oil system components

1972-1974 circuit board cover

Alternator

The 022.903.023 three-phase 50-Amp alternator used on all four-cylinder 914s was also found on VW 411, 412 and period Transporter models. It was incorporated with the cooling fan and belt-driven. It was updated with a newer model with the same output in 1975.

The 770-Watt Bosch alternator on the 914-6 was the one used on period 911s. It was attached to the engine cooling fan and belt-driven.

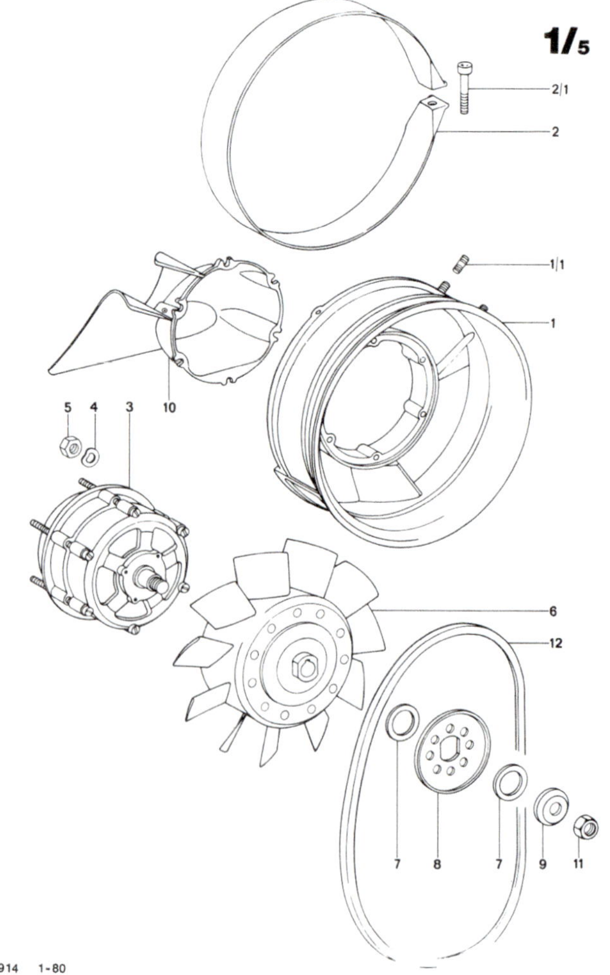

Illustration 1/5 showing 914-6 fan and alternator set up

Fan and alternator on the 914-4 were hidden by engine components and shrouds

Voltage Regulators

Four-cylinder car voltage regulators changed only once in mid-1973 and were the same for all engine models and displacements during those times.

043.903.803 B – early
021.903.803 A – late

The newer regulator was first installed on the following engines:

W	0 192 030
EA	0 070 362
EB	0 003 373
GA	0 001 675
GB	0 002 583
GC	0 000 001
AN	0 000 001
EC	0 000 001

The 914-6 regulator was located in the same location as on the 914-4, but was specific to that model. The 1972 914-6 used the early 043.903.803 B regulator used on the 914-4.

Fuel Injection Control Box

All 914-4s with fuel injection had an electronic control box located between the battery and firewall. There were 7 types:

1970 US
1970 RoW
1971-1973 1.7 and 2.0
1974 1.8
1974 2.0 US and 1974-1976 RoW
1975 1.8
1975-1976 2.0 US

Electronic Ignition 914-6

All 914-6s had an electronic ignition unit in the same location as the fuel injection box in the 914-4. The GT with twin ignition was a little more elaborate.

Fuel injection control box 1971-1973

The control box was relocated when air-conditioning was fitted. 1974 2.0 US

1975-1976 US fuel injection control box

914-6 ignition box

Dual ignition 914-6 GT system

The distributor and coil were on the right side of the 914-4 engine

Coil & Distributor

There were three coils used on four-cylinder cars.

	Part Number	Bosch Number
1970	022.905.115	
1971-1973 1.7, 2.0	022.905.115 A	0.221.102.076
1974-1976 1.8 US		
1974-1976 1.8 Euro, 2.0	021.905.115 A	

The coil was relocated in 1974

Four-cylinder distributors were a little more complicated.

	Part Number	Bosch Number
1970-1972 1.7 US	022.905.205 F	0 231 174 007
1970-1973 Euro	022.905.205 H	0 231 163 011
1973 1.7 US	022.905.205 P	0 231 168 005
1973-1976 2.0 except California	039.905.205 A	0 231 174 011
1973-1976 2.0 California	039.905.205 B	0 231 172 021
1974-1976 1.8 US	021.905.205 A	0 231 167 018
1974-1976 1.8 Euro carbureted	022.905.205 S	0 231 170 093

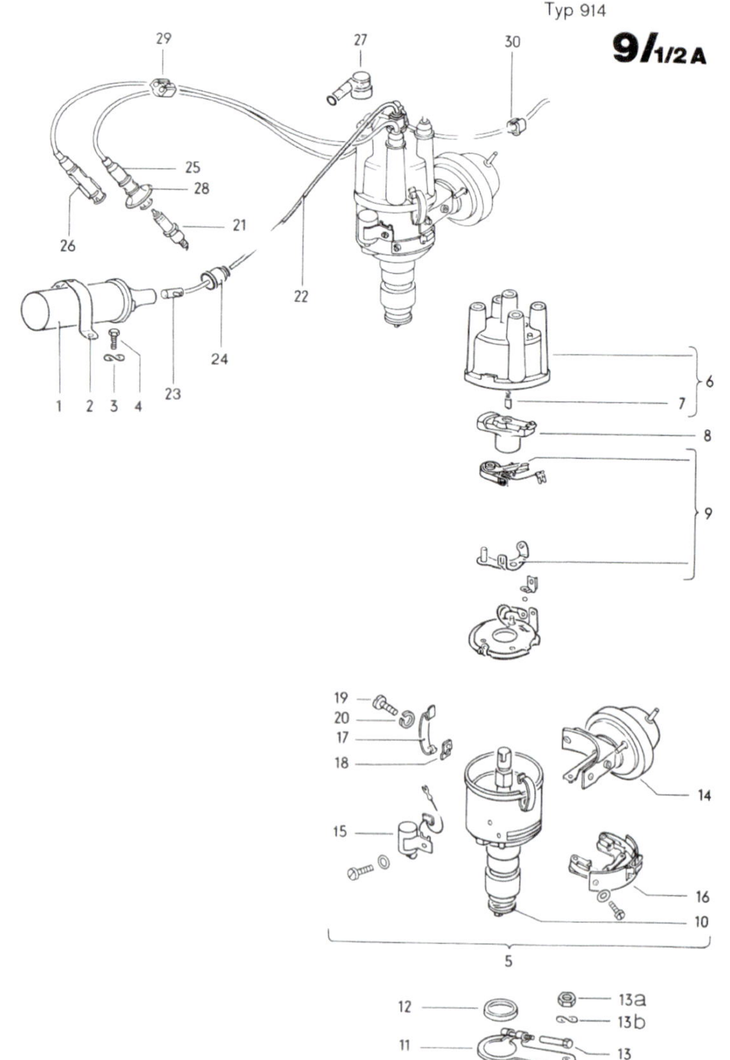

Illustration 9/1/2A ignition system 914-4

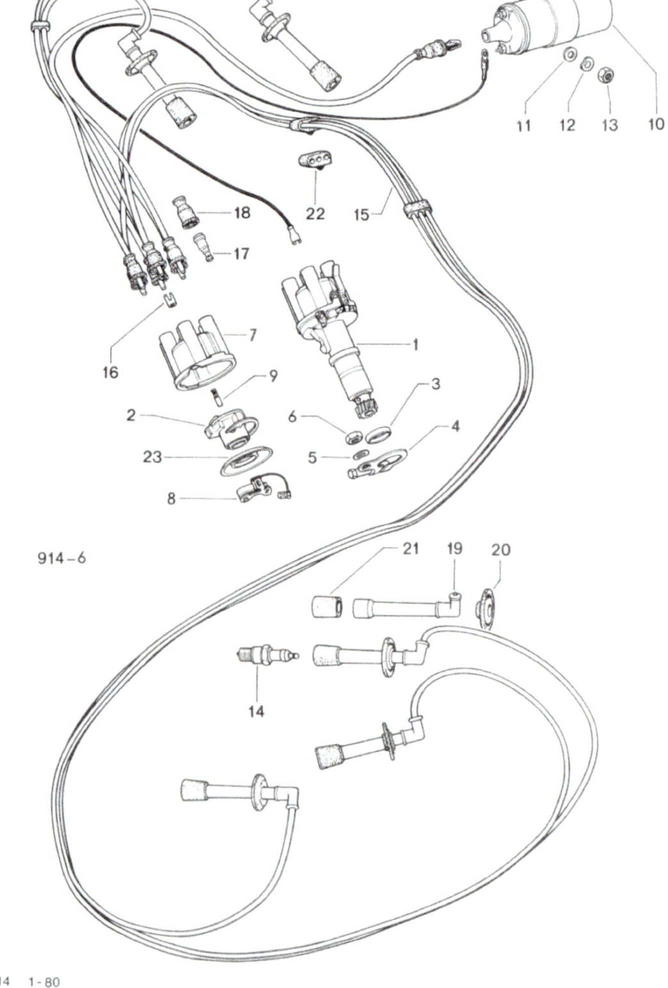

Illustration 9/1/2 ignition system 914-6

The coil on the 914-6 mounted to the fan housing. The distributor is obscurred by the fan shrouding

The 1970 914-6 was fitted with a Marelli distributor. 1971-1972 cars had Bosch distributors. Both distributors used the same Bosch coil. They also had the same (Marelli) part number in later parts manuals indicating that the Bosch distributor was not available in later years.

Marelli distributor	911.602.022.00
Bosch distributor	901.602.021.05
Coil	901.602.502.00

Starter

Three different starters were used on 914 models.

	Part Number	Bosch Number
914-6	923.604.191.00	
914 1.7/1.8	003.911.023 B	0.001.212.005
914 2.0	039.911.023	0.001.212.012

The starter bolted to the transmission bell housing

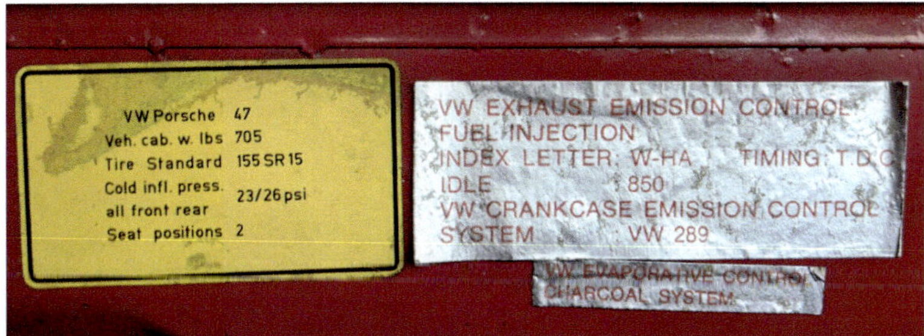

Tire pressure/capacities and emissions stickers mounted on firewall, 1970-1971

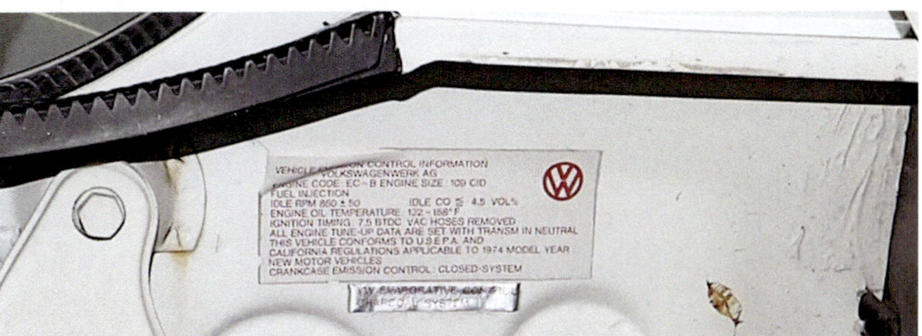

The location of the timing/emissions and charcoal system stickers 1973-1976

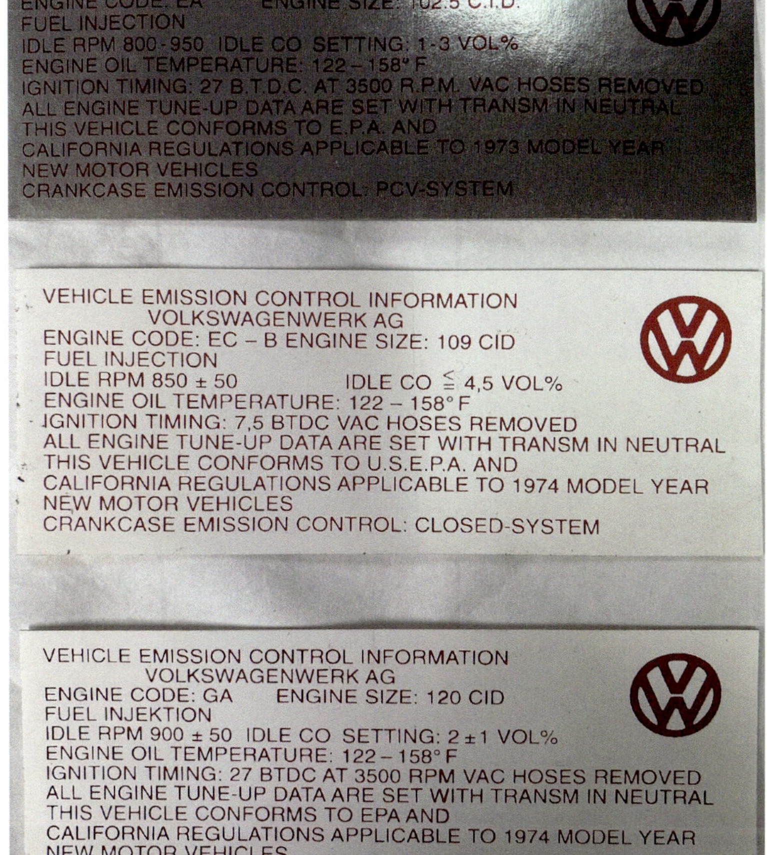

Timing/emissions sticker 1973 1.7 top, 1974 1.8 center and 1974 2.0 bottom

Decals/Stickers

On the left front firewall in the engine compartment of the US spec. 1970-1971 914-4 was a gold foil tire pressure/capacities sticker, a silver timing/emissions sticker and silver charcoal system sticker. The same emissions stickers were in this location in 1972, but the tire pressure/capacities sticker moved to the fuel tank (*see page 60*).

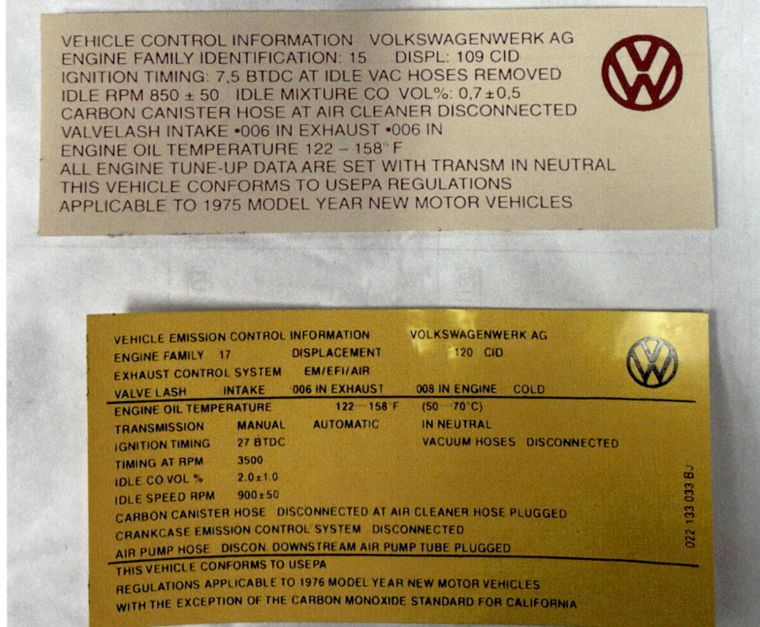

Timing emissions sticker 1975 1.8 top and 1976 2.0 below

The later timing/emission stickers were specific to the engine type fitted and were located on the left side wall except the 1975 1.8, which was on the left front impeller housing. The 1973 sticker was silver, 1974 was white, 1975 off-white and the 1976 version yellow. Lettering was red/except on the the 1976, which had black lettering. All of these had small silver charcoal system stickers below with red lettering.

Four-cylinder cars also had a valve adjustment sticker located on the left front fan shroud. The one for 1.7 and 1.8 cars was white with red or black letters, while the one for 2.0 cars was silver with red letters.

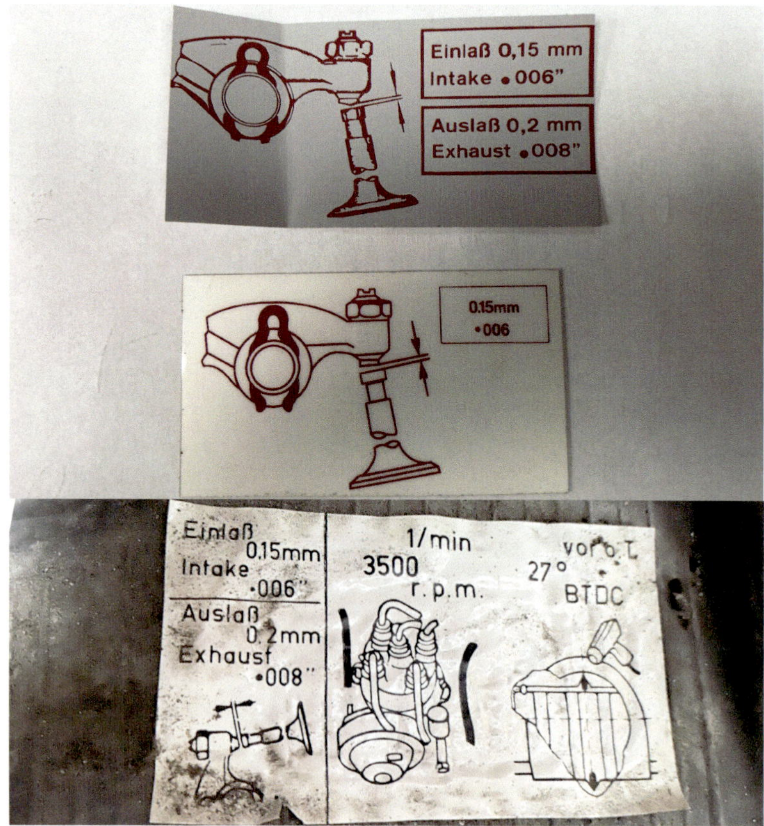

Valve adjustment stickers top to bottom: 2.0, 1.7, 1.8

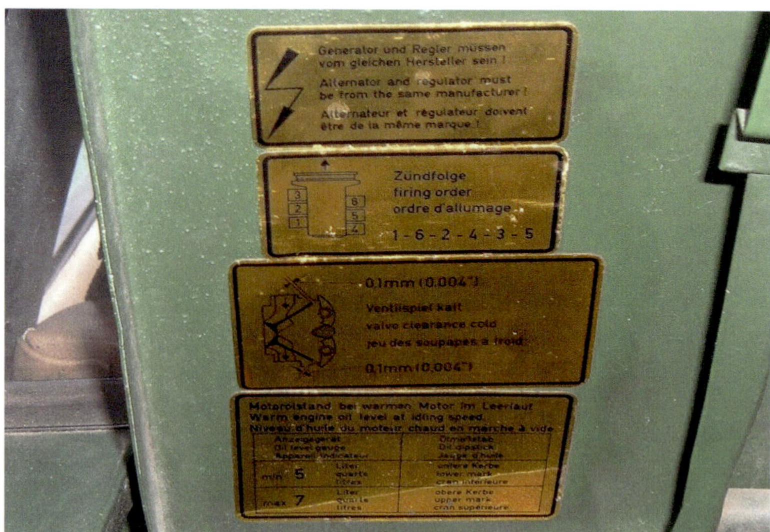

Original gold foil stickers were somewhat casually applied on the 914-6

914-6 tire pressure sticker was on the right side of the engine lid

The 914-6 had gold foil stickers for various functions on the inside of the rear lid. On the driver's side from top to bottom they were: Alternator, Firing Order, Valve Adjustment and Oil Level. On the passenger's side there was a Tire Pressure sticker.

As with 911s, the foil timing stickers were located on the fan housing on all 914-6s.

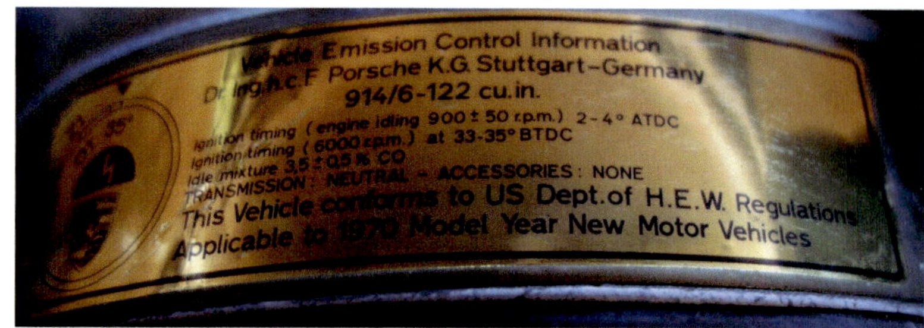

Timing sticker 1970 914-6

Timing sticker 1971 914-6. Note coil mounting

Oil filler necks 911 above and 914-6 below

Oil System 914-6

The 914-6 had a dry sump system like its 911 progenitor. The remote oil tank was on the left side of the 914, as opposed to the right on the 911. Along with a separate version for cars equipped with Sportomatic transmission, the tanks were unique to this model. The oil filler cap was accessible through the engine lid and oil level dipstick was located in the neck under the cap. The tank was not modified during production. All 914 bodies were stamped to accommodate this tank.

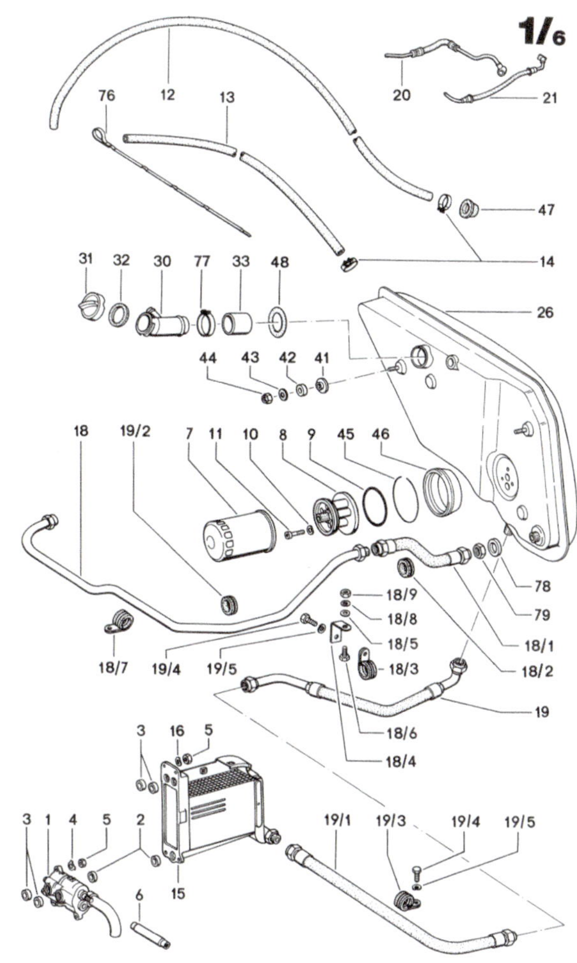

Illustration 1/6, 914-6 oil system including cooler

Dry sump oil filler location 914-6

Heater Blower Motor

1970-1972 914-4 models have a supplemental electric blower motor that mounts to the top of the impeller housing. The plastic hoses that are attached on each side tap into the heat system via additional ducting at the heat exchanger.

In 1973 a higher volume motor was introduced that had a single outlet and was mounted to a metal bracket welded to the left front en-

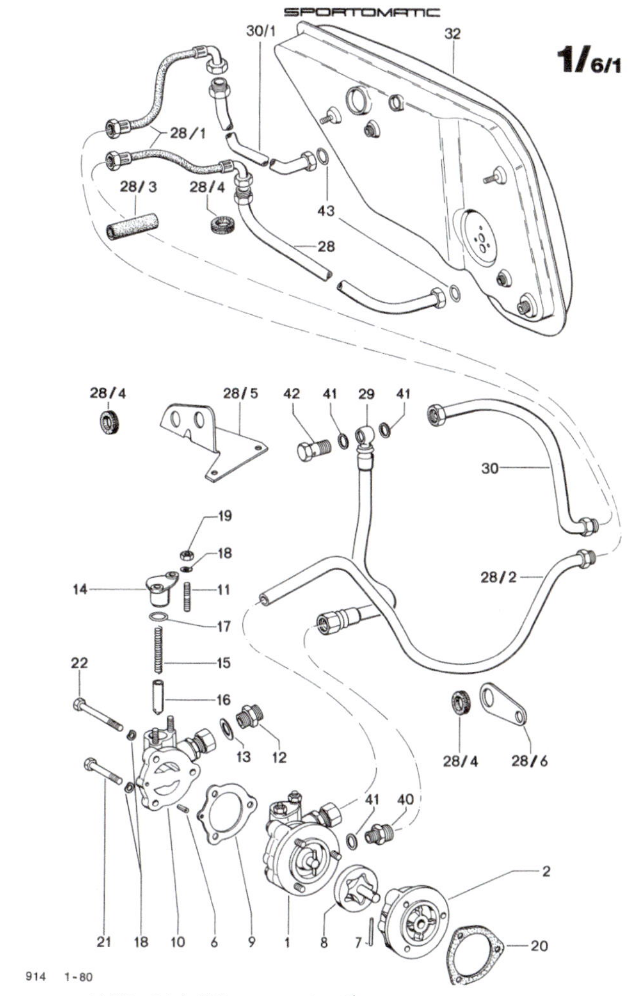

Illustration 1/6/1, 914-6 Sportomatic oil system

Original dual-hose fan

Final style dual-hose fan

gine bay shelf. From 1973 through early 1975, the air was routed through the left heat exchange and the ducting to the right side was capped. From late 1975 through the end of production the air was again routed to both heat exchangers.

The 914-6, which used the large engine cooling fan to blow air through the heat exchangers, did not require the supplemental fan.

The heat valve located in front of the heat exchanger

Interim single-hose fan

Heater Valves

All four-cylinder cars used the same heat valves, which came in left and right sides. The ones for the 914-6 were also sided and were specific for this model, since they incorporated a hole in the bell cap to vent heat to lessen vapor lock.

1/18 A

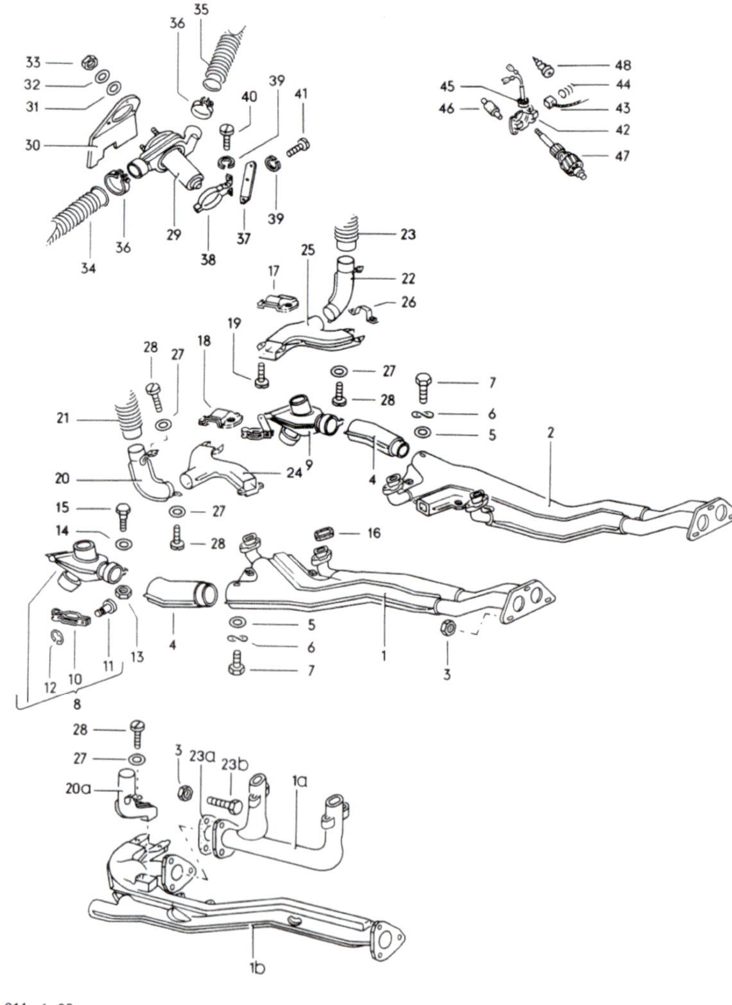

Illustration 1/18A, 914-4 heating system

Heat Exchangers

Heat exchangers are the way that most air-cooled engines produced heat for the interior occupants during cold weather. Gasoline heaters optional in other Porsche models were never offered on 914s.

Many four-cylinder 914s today are fitted with stainless steel heat exchangers that come in two basic types. One fits 2.0 models and the other the 1.7 and 1.8s. Original heat exchangers were not stainless and deteriorated rapidly from a combination of high temperature and condensation.

The same two types of heat exchangers were fitted originally. The external appearance of the ones for the small displacement cars was unmodified on cars not sold in the US throughout production. The internal diameter (ID) of the pipes was 29 mm on the 1.7s and 33 mm on the 1.8s. In the US they were used 1970-1974. Since they were originally designed to incorporate a standard VW muffler, they were angled upward at the back.

The 2.0 heat exchangers were different at the muffler end, having a flatter pathway to the Porsche designed muffler. Though the internal diameter of the pipes was 34 mm, the exhaust flanges were different from the ones for the 1.7 and 1.8 models. Like the latter, they were used throughout production except on 1975-1976 US spec. 2.0s.

The 1975 and 1976 US-bound cars had unique two-piece heat exchangers due to emission reducing mandates. Unlike the previous versions, these incorporated a two-into-one exhaust pathway with provision for exhaust recirculation. Both 1.8 and 2.0 versions used the same system with 39 mm ID pipes.

For the 914-6 the two additional cylinders necessitated a totally different set of heat exchangers.

Muffler

The mufflers, tail pipes and muffler brackets loosely corresponded to the four different types of heat exchangers described above.

The 1.7 liter four-cylinder muffler (021.251.101 E) with separate tail pipe originally was used from 1970-1972. The muffler was made by Leistritz and was also used on the VW bus/transporter (with different, right exiting tail pipe). A longer tail pipe was installed when the valance was modified in 1972. A one-year-only 1973 muffler (021.251.101 K) was used featuring a left side exiting short tail pipe.

1/8

914 1-80

Illustration 1/8, 914-6 heating and exhaust systems

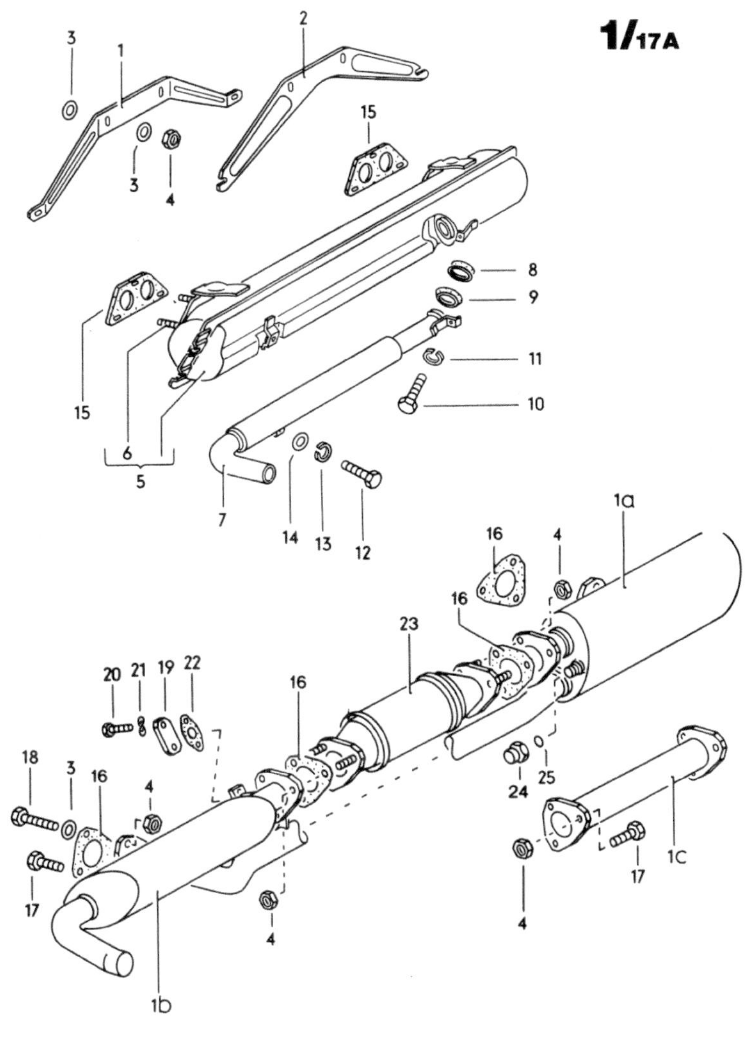

Illustration 1/17A, 914-4 mufflers

Stainless steel replacement heat exchangers have original configuration on this 1973 2.0. Note also muffler hanger bracket

Original heat exchangers and muffler from 1975-1976. California spec. cars had a catalytic converter where the pipe connecting the mufflers is located

Heat exchanger/muffler joint area 1.7/1.8 (left) and 2.0 (right)

The above two mufflers were phased out and replaced by one (021.251.053 C) in 1974 which could be retrofitted to all 1.7 and 1.8 powered cars. It continued to be used until the end of production excluding 1975-1976 US spec. models described below. This muffler was much different in construction and featured a tail pipe that was secured with three bolts and exited from the left side. All of the above used a single muffler hanger bracket (022.251.067 A).

The two-liter cars built for the US market for 1973-1974 and 1973-1976 for the non-US market 2.0s used a second type of muffler (039.251.051 D). It was not illustrated in the parts manual, but more closely resembled the one used on the 914-6, having an integral tailpipe. A chrome removable tip is listed in the parts manual, but was not fitted on new cars. The hanger bracket was used only on this muffler.

The final four-cylinder engine muffler was used on all 1975-1976 US spec. cars, regardless of displacement. The three-piece muffler system consisted of a primary muffler, connecting pipe and secondary muffler. In California-bound cars, the connecting pipe was replaced with a catalytic converter. The hanger bracket was again unique for this system.

The 914-6 muffler resembled the one used on contemporary 911s, but it was made specifically for the 914, having a unique tail pipe bend. Like the 911 there was a chrome removeable tip. Once again, the hanger bracket was model specific, but closely resembled the one used on the 2.0 above.

Early style mffler with separate tail pipe

021.251.053C muffler with tail pipe secured by three bolts

2.0 muffler resembled a 914-6 muffler

914-6 muffler with removable chrome tip

Brakes, Suspension and Transmission

Brakes, 914-4

All 914 Porsches had disc brakes front and rear. Four-cylinder cars had rotors which accommodated four lug bolts per wheel as used on contemporary VW 411 models. The 11.05-inch VW rotors, which could be used on either side, changed in June 1972 at chassis number 472 291 9033. These had a different offset and were designed to be used with the calipers described below. In January 1973 at chassis number 473 291 2511 a third rotor was introduced. This final rotor variety incorporated a wheel-centering ring, which made it easier to mount and balance the wheels.

The first generation front brakes

Centering ring on the final front rotor

Early caliper with single bleeder valve

Second caliper with two bleeder valves

Front calipers came in left and right sides. There was a single change and it coincided with the initial rotor change in June 1972. The newer version incorporated dual bleeder valves and accommodated thicker 14 mm brake pads. Earlier ones were 10 mm.

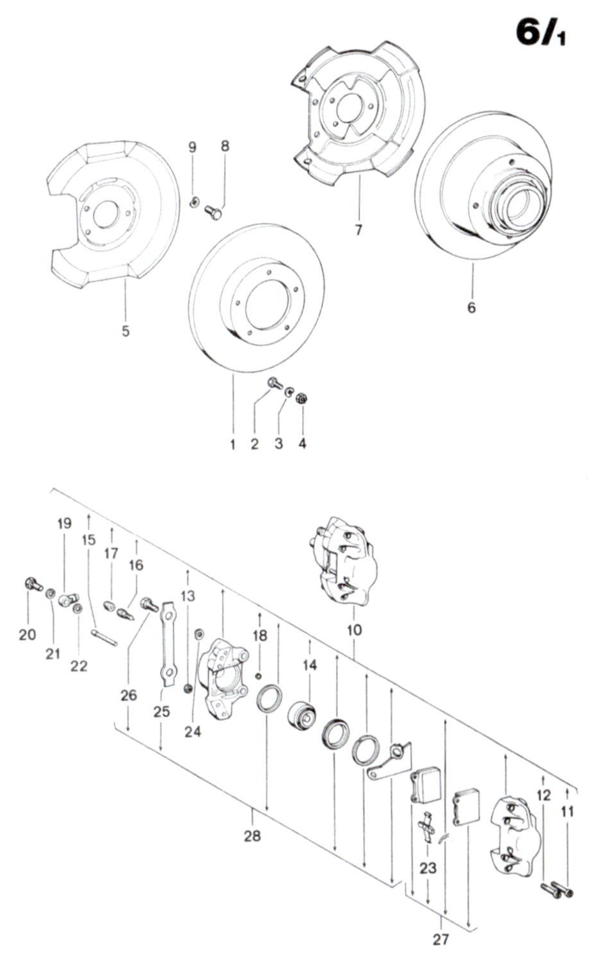

Illustration 6/1, front brake 914-4. tRotor with centering disc right (#6)

Early rear brake and caliper, 914-4

Late rear brake and caliper, 914-4

Rear rotors and calipers were unique to the four-cylinder 914s and were not shared with other makes or models. Calipers were again sided and 11.10-inch rotors were not. The parking brake, unlike the 911, was incorporated into the caliper. Rear calipers were modified to include dual bleeder valves around the time the front calipers were modified.

Brakes, 914-6

The 914-6 also featured four-wheel disc brakes, but they were not the same as the ones on four-cylinder cars. The hubs incorporated five wheel-mounting studs like contemporary 911s. Front rotors on the 914-6 were the 11.12-inch ventilated ones, first used on the 1967 911S. As with other rotors, they were exchangeable side to side.

The calipers used were also from the 911 parts bin and were the ones first used on the 1967 911S. Again, left and right calipers were fitted and they did not change during the three year production run.

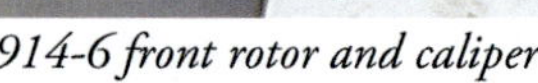

914-6 front rotor and caliper

914-6 front caliper and vented rotor

914-6 rear rotor and caliper

914-6 rear caliper and solid rotor

As on the four-cylinder car, rear rotors and calipers were unique to the 914-6 and were not shared with other makes or models. Calipers were again sided and the 11.25-inch solid rotors were not. The parking brake was also incorporated into the caliper.

Brakes 914-6 GT and 916

The 916 used the same setup as the 914-6 up front, except the calipers were replaced by the ones fitted to the contemporary 911S. The 914-6 GT went a step farther using the calipers developed for the racing versions of the 911 (901.351.047.13 and 901.351.048.13).

Both 914-6 GT and 916 used ventilated rear rotors that were unique to those models. They also had modified rear 914-6 calipers with a spacer added to accommodate the added width of the rotors. Some later GTs had rotors similar to period 911s, which had drum style parking brake shoes inside the rotor.

Master Cylinder

All 914s were fitted with dual circuit brakes, which included a tandem master cylinder with dual pistons.

6/1/1

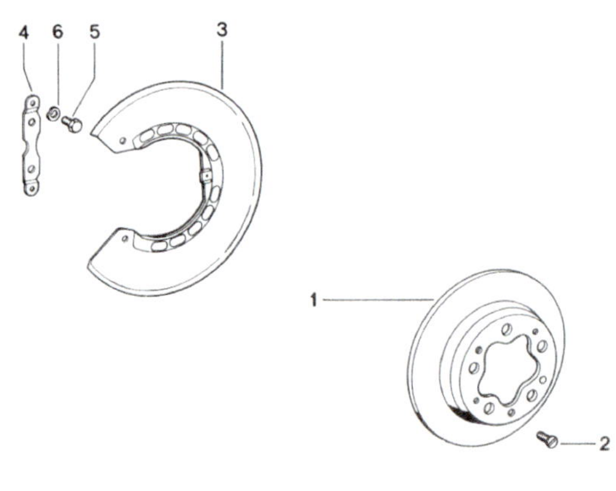

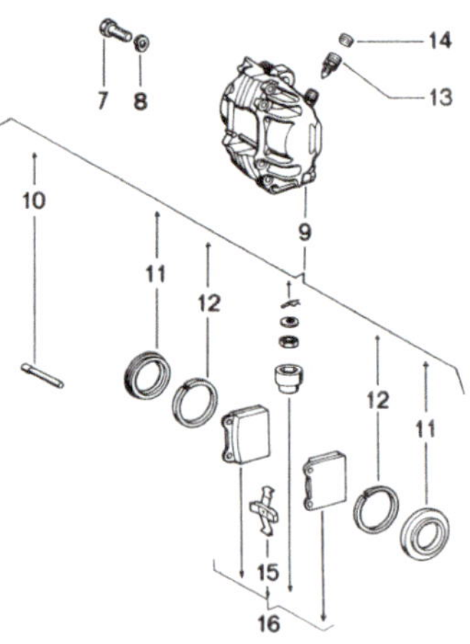

914 1-80

Illustration 6/1/1, front brake 914-6

There were two different master cylinders for both the 914-4 and the 914-6. The difference between the cylinders was the presence or absence of a brake warning light switch which detected loss of pressure in the system. US spec. cars always had the warning light (*see pages 64-65*).

The main difference between the 914-4 and 914-6 cylinders was the internal diameter. The four-cylinder diameter was 17.46 mm, while the six was 19.05 mm. The larger diameter cylinder was associated with larger piston size in the 914-6 calipers.

Other Brake System Items

The white plastic reservoir was subtly different between four and six-cylinder cars and had differing part numbers.

A brake pressure regulator to help keep the rear brakes from locking before the front ones was fitted to all 914s. It was mounted to the front lower left firewall on the driver's side. They varied between four and six-cylinder cars. The one for the four was modified in March 1974 at chassis number 474 291 5752.

Brake fluid reservoir was mounted to the left of the fuel tank

Front Suspension and Steering

The 914 utilized front suspension components that mirrored those on contemporary 911s. The lower A-frames on the 914-6 were the same ones used on 911s, while the ones on the 914-4 were unique to that model. Neither version was modified during production. The ones found on GTs were of heavier construction for added strength.

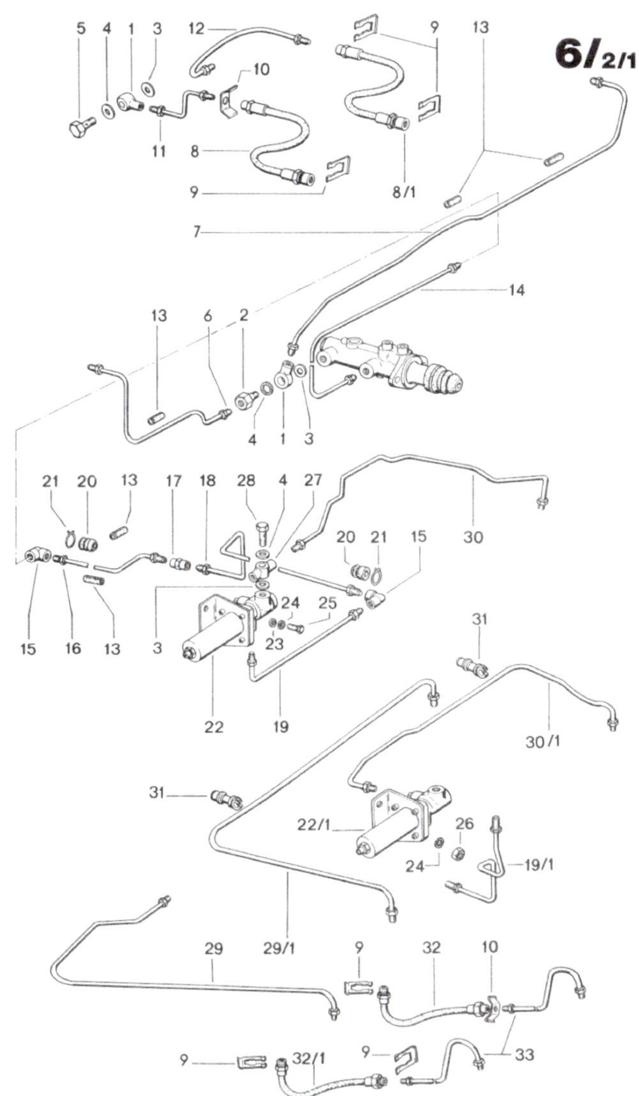

Illustration 6/2/1, brake lines.Pressure regulators are numbers 22 and 22/1

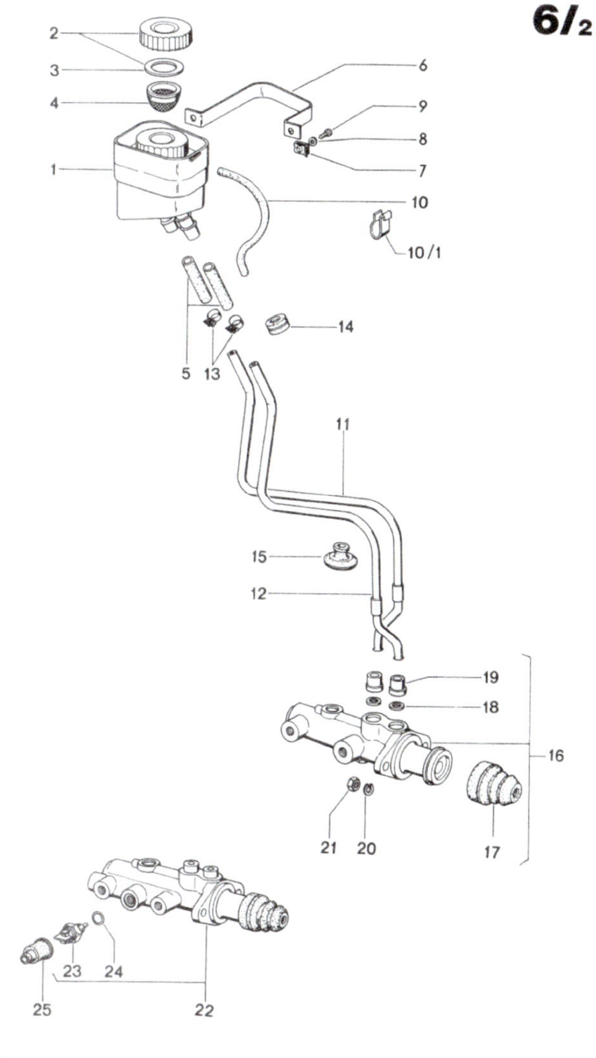

Illustration 6/2, reservoir and master cylinder. Lower has warning light switch

The 24" (610 mm) torsion bars were the same length as the ones on the 911, but were 17.9 mm diameter. As with the A-frames, four and six-cylinder versions were different with the ones on the 914-4 having 29 splines and the ones on the 914-6 having 30. They were never modified.

The front struts again resembled the ones used on period 911s incorporating the shock absorber and front spindle. They were sided and secured to the lower A-frame with a ball joint at the bottom. There were again different units for four and six-cylinder cars and all that were made by Boge had replaceable shock absorber inserts. The four-cylinder struts were gray and the six-cylinder ones, generally black.

At the same point that brakes were altered in June 1972 at chassis number 472 291 9033 on four-cylinder 914s, the lower ball joints were updated. Green painted Bilstein struts were first offered at this time as optional equipment and these shock absorber inserts were not replaceable.

Both Koni & Bilstein strut configurations were available on GT models. GTs and 916s also used the period 911S struts which were configured to use the larger calipers.

Front strut and A-frame arrangement was similar to period 911s. Anti-sway bar linkage can be seen in the right side photo

A ZF steering rack with a 17.8:1 ratio and just over 3 turns lock to lock was used on all 914s. The steering column with double u-joints like the 911 would have been easily adapted for RHD.

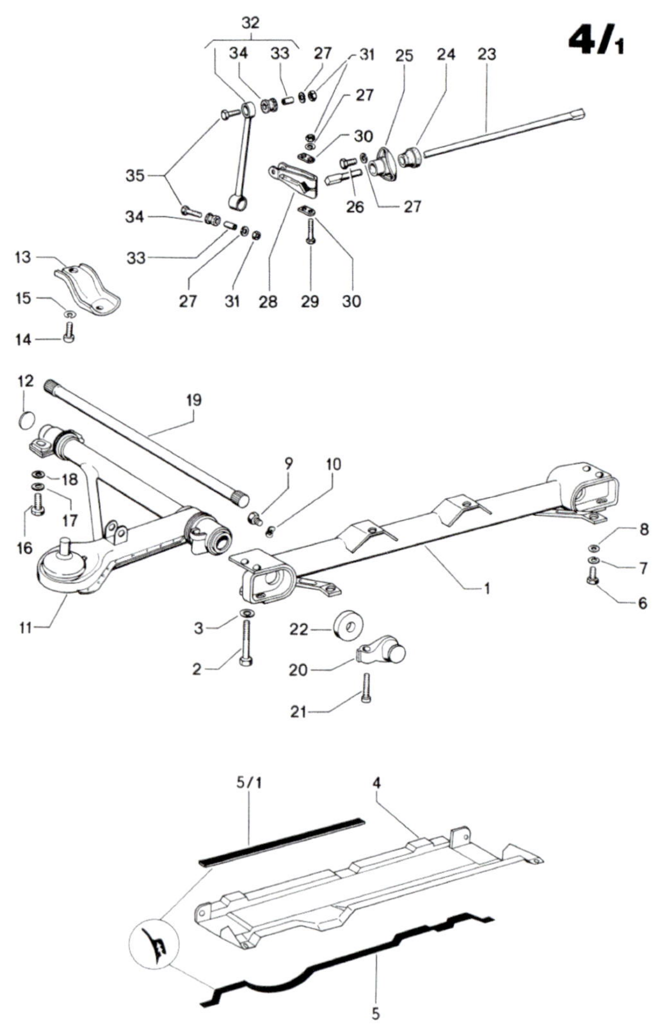

914 1-80

Illustration 4/1, front suspension and anti-sway bar

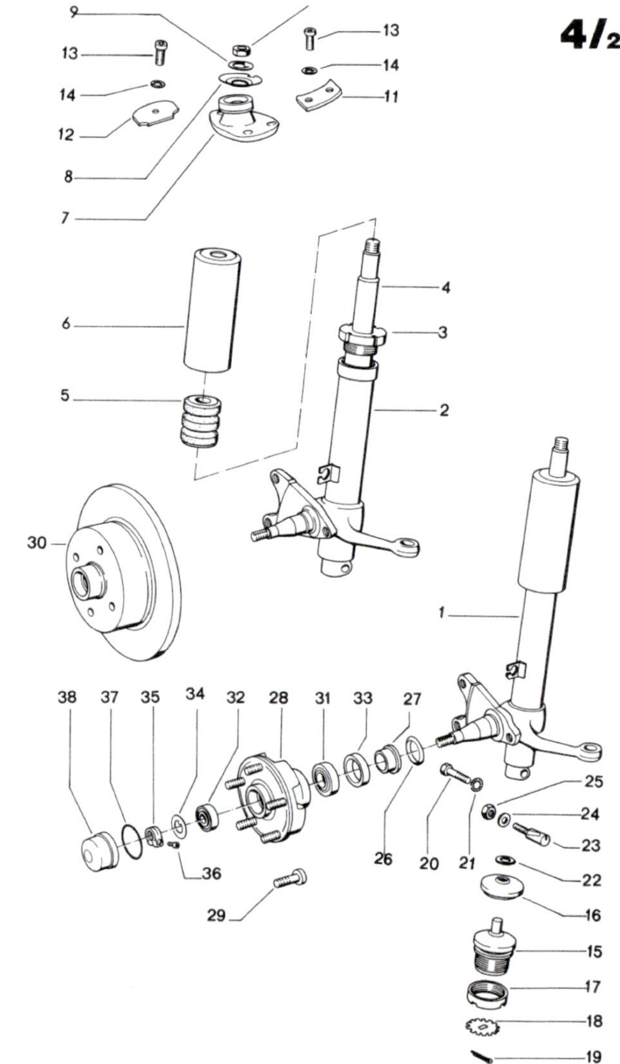

914 1-80

Illustration 4/2, front brake, strut and hub

Rear anti-sway bar and linkage

Rear Suspension

A trailing arm suspension with coil springs was selected because engine position would not allow a torsion bar setup. This was the first use of coil springs on any Porsche model.

The left trailing arm is different on the 914-6 because the bracket that held the emergency brake cable had to be angled so that the cable did not touch the heat exchanger. The right side is the same on all 914s.

On the GT and 916, chassis strengthening plates were welded to the chassis for lateral loading caused by the higher power and wider tires. On the GT the spring mounts were also beefed up.

Similar to those up front, coil-over Boge shocks were standard on early 914s with different unsided varieties for four and six-cylinder cars. Optional Bilstein rear shocks were fitted as a set along with front ones.

Anti-Sway Bars

The 1972 914-6 was the first 914 to offer optional sway bars. 1973-1976 914s also had optional sway bars, but no 1972 4-cylinder cars had them. They were standard on the 1973 US spec. 2.0, on all Limited Edition models and incorporated into other option packages.

The configuration of the bars was similar to contemporary 911 bars with the front sway bars being the actual ones used on 911s.

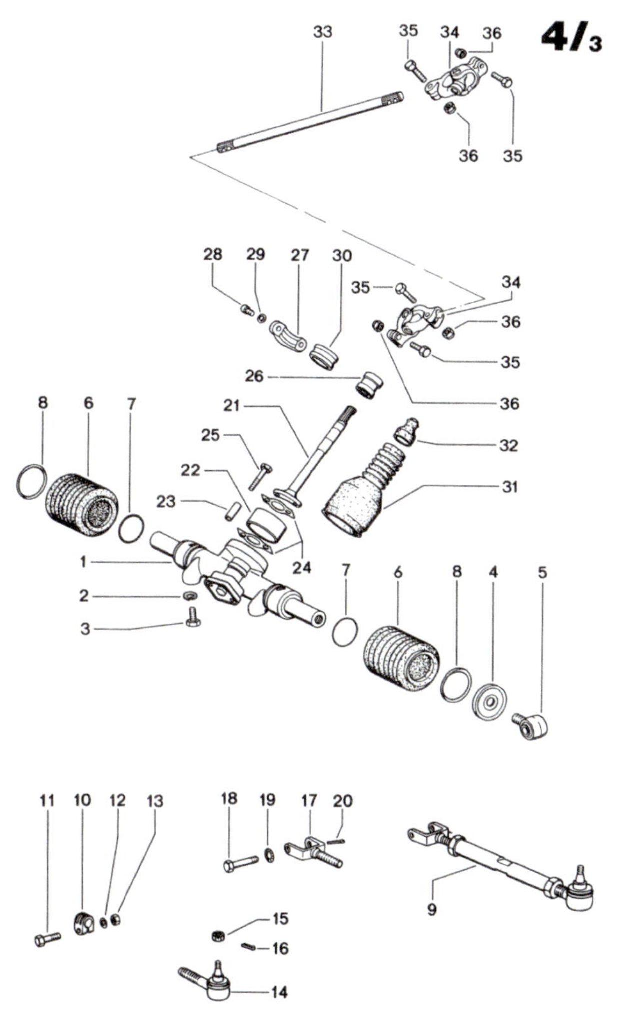

Illustration 4/3, steering

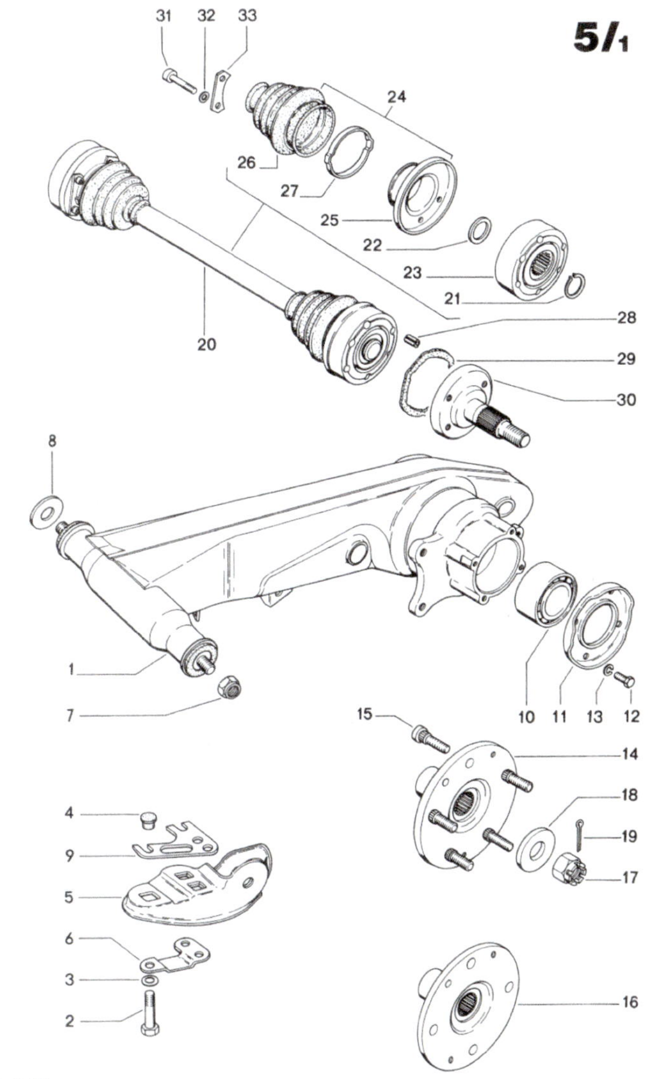

Illustration 5/1, rear suspension

914-4 spring with two green lines

Four-cylinder cars had 15 mm front and 16 mm rear to correct understeer. The 914-6 had 16 mm front and 15 mm rear to correct oversteer. One GT configuration available included 14 mm front and 16 mm rear.

After 1973, many cars not equipped with sway bars had the mounting brackets for them installed on the A-frames.

914 Rear Coil Springs

The 914 parts manual lists three rear springs which have different spring rates for both four and six-cylinder 914s. While it is obvious that these were originally fitted in pairs, there is no explanation if there was any pattern to when they were originally fitted.

Part Number	Application	Coding*	Wire Diam.	Free Length	Rate lbs/in
914.333.531.04 xxx	914-4**		9.6 mm	461mm	
914.333.531.11.201	914-4	1 line	9.6 mm	471 mm	52.45
914.333.531.11.202	914-4	2 lines	9.6 mm	471 mm	53.94
914.333.531.11.203	914-4	3 lines	9.6 mm	471 mm	55.43
914.333.531.05.101	914-6	1 line	10 mm	431 mm	58
914.333.531.05.102	914-6	2 lines	10 mm	431 mm	60
914.333.531.05.103	914-6	3 lines	10 mm	431 mm	62
914.333.531.07	914-6 GT	Med	10.6 mm		80
914.333.531.08	914-6 GT	Soft	10.4 mm		70
914.333.531.09	914-6 GT	Hard	10.6 mm		90

*Lines were green on 914-4 and yellow on 914-6

**Starting with chassis number 472 291 7885, the spring length was increased from 461 mm to 471 mm

5/2

914 1-80

Illustration 5/2, rear spring and anti-sway bar

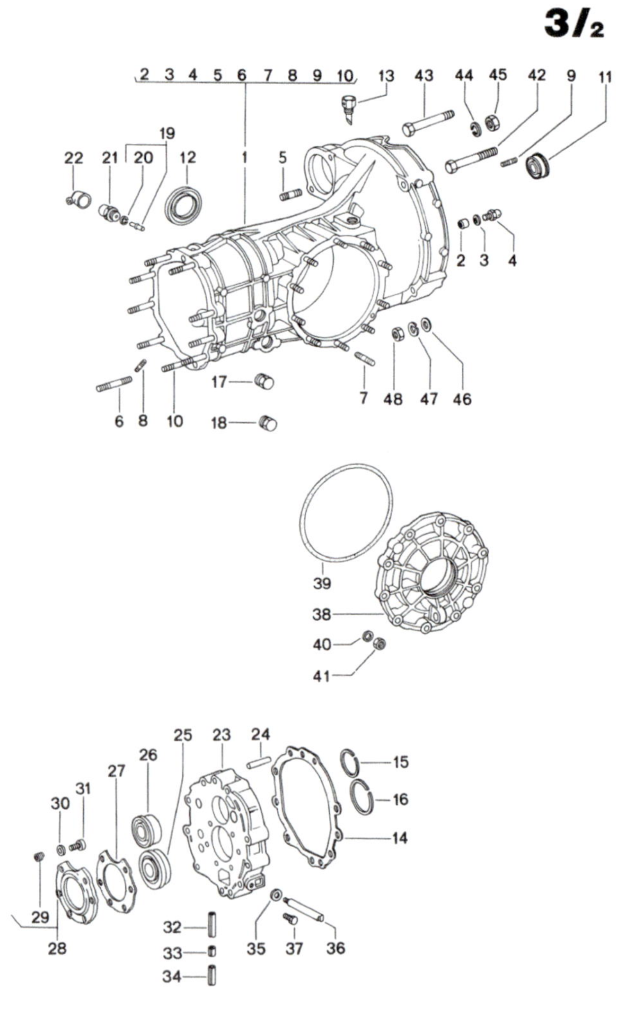

Illustration 3/2, five-speed transmission housing

Transmission

All standard 914s came with five-speed gearboxes. Differing gear ratios were fitted to four and six-cylinder cars — listed below and on the following page. All five-speed 914s had a 7:31 final drive ratio.

Optional Sportomatic gearboxes, which offered clutch-less shifting via a torque converter and four forward gears, were available 1970-1971 only on 914-6s. Between five and 25 were built. One privately researched account lists four US spec. cars and sixteen European cars so equipped. Sportomatics shared virtually no common components with manual transmission 914s and had a final drive ratio of 7:27.

Another rare option was a limited slip or *locking* differential. The parts manual indicates that it was avilable on any model with a five-speed gearbox, but was apparently only installed on 1970 and 1971 914-4 models. Those gearboxes numbers begin with *HB* and based on the sequential numbers issued, only three were fitted in 1970.

On October 1, 1972 a new numbering system was introduced behginning with HA followed by the dd/mm/y format meaning that all gearboxes produced on the same day had the same number.

A single change was made to the five-speed gearbox. This was at the 1973 model year and was made in response to criticism about the imprecise linkage on the original 914/11 gearbox. On the earlier cars

Five-speed gearbox with tail shift.

with this 914/11 gearbox, the linkage rod exited from the left side of the tail cover. When the shift linkage was first developed for the 914, all 911 components were used, even though the linkage had to now engage three feet further back, resulting in a vague and sloppy feel.

The 1973-1976 so-called *side shift* 914/12 gearbox was modified to shift from the lower left driver's side, just behind the differential. The shift forks and tail cover were changed to eliminate the older *tail shift* arrangement. This resulted in a much more precise, less complicated assembly and eliminated complaints about the vagueness of the 914 shifter.

Standard Gear Ratios 914-4 – all years and engines

Gear	Teeth	Ratio
First	11/34	3.091
Second	18/32	1.778
Third	23/28	1.217
Fourth	27/25	0.926
Fifth	29/22	0.759

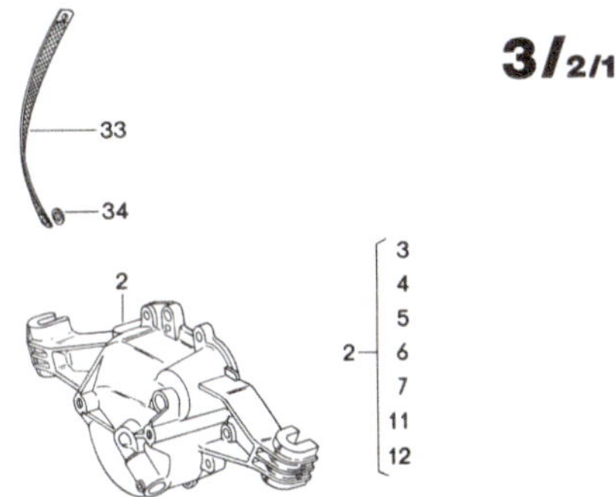

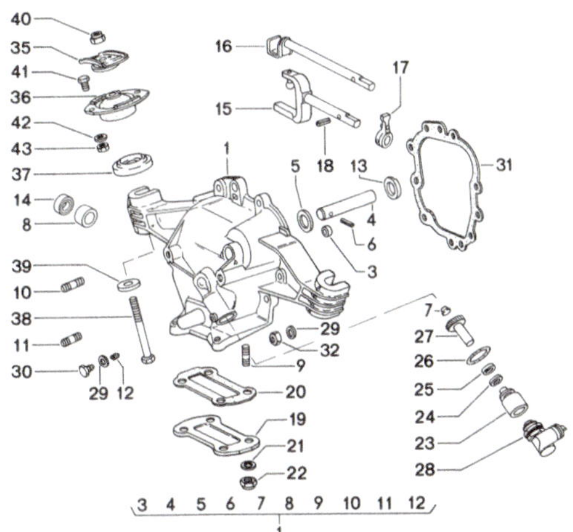

Illustration 4/1, tail shift tail cover below, side shift above

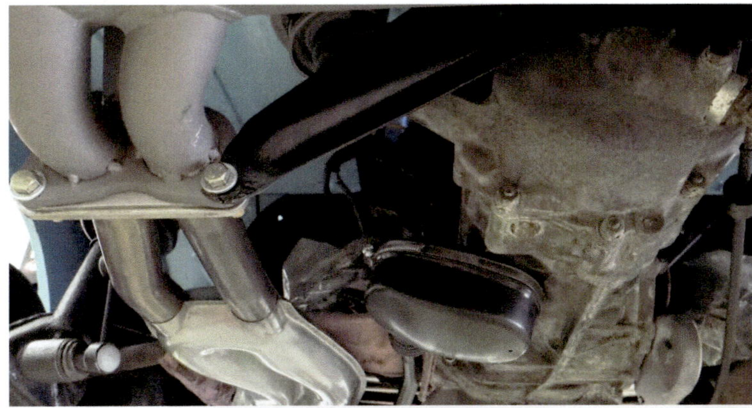

Side shift linkage first used for the 1973 model year. Removing the linkage cover the shift mechanism is revealed

Standard Gear Ratios 914-6 – all years

Gear	Teeth	Ratio
First	11/34	3.091
Second	18/34	1.758
Third	23/29	1.218
Fourth	27/25	0.926
Fifth	31/22	0.710

Gear Ratios Sportomatic

Gear	Teeth	Ratio
First	15/36	2.400
Second	20/31	1.550
Third	24/27	1.125
Fourth	28/24	0.857

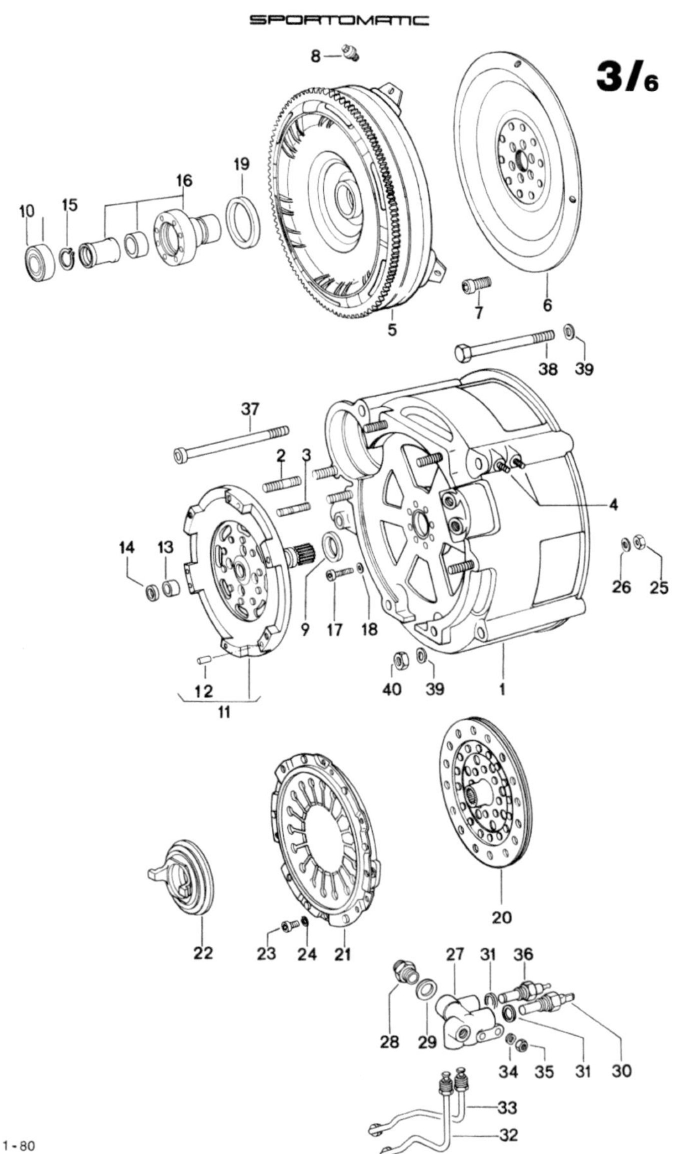

Illustration 3/6, Sportomatic torque converter mechanism

Other Transmission Related Components

Twin disc-shaped rubber gearbox mounts were located at the tail cover of the gearbox at the rear of the car. All 914-6 cars including those equipped with Sportomatic transmissions used the same mounts. Four-cylinder cars had slightly softer ones.

The speedometer drive gear was also located on the rear transmission case. It drove a cable which ran all the way to the speedometer. Drive gears were the same on all models, including Sportomatics.

Half shafts, which connected the differential to the rear hubs had constant velocity joints at either end, as fitted to period 911s. As with many other components, the ones on four and six-cylinder cars differed. No changes occurred during production.

For the 914-6 GT an external oil pump was occasionally added to better lubricate the somewhat delicate 914/11 gearbox from the added power. A differing solution for the same problem was accomplished by re-engineering components of the 915 gearbox from the 1972 911, using the 915 case with unique tail cover and shift forks for the eleven 916 models produced. This gearbox had a different shift pattern (*see page 80*).

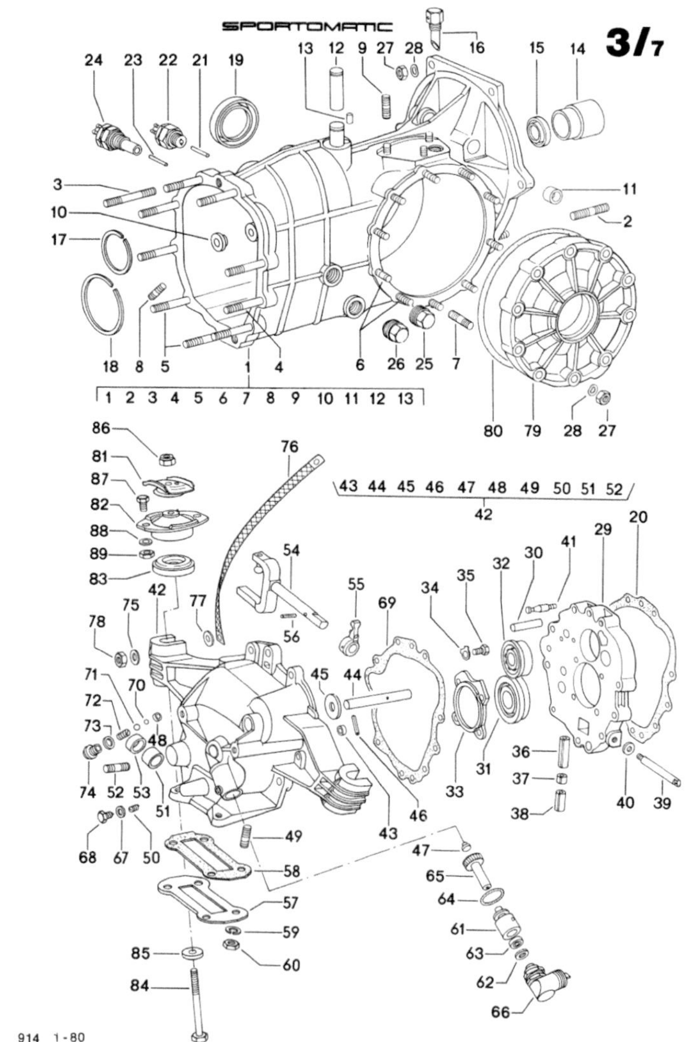

Illustration 3/7, unique, rare Sportomatic transmission housing

Appendices

Chassis, Engine and Transmission Data

Year Mfg.	Model Year	Official Model Design.	Engine Designation Official	Internal	Displ. cc.	Horse-power (DIN)-RPM	Stroke & Bore	Compr. Ratio	Fuel System Type
1969/ 1970	1970	914-4	1.7	W	1679	80@ 4900	66/90	8.2:1	MPC
		914-6	2.0	901/36 901/37 901/38 901/39	1991	110@ 5800	66/80	8.6:1	Weber
1970/ 1971	1971	914-4	1.7	W	1679	80@ 4900	66/90	8.2:1	MPC
		914-6	2.0	901/36 901/37 901/38 901/39	1991	110@ 5800	66/80	8.6:1	Weber
1971/ 1972	1972	914-4	1.7	W	1679	80@ 4900	66/90	8.2:1	MPC
				EA		80@ 4900		8.2:1	MPC
		914-6	2.0	901/36	1991	110@ 5800	66/80	8.6:1	Weber
		916	2.4	901/56	2341	190@ 6500	70/84	8.5:1	Mechanical Fuel Injection
1972/ 1973	1973	914	1.7	W	1679	80@ 4900	66/90	8.2:1	MPC
				EA		80@ 4900		8.2:1	MPC
				EB		72@ 5000		7.3:1	MPC
			2.0	GA	1971	95@ 4900	71/94	7.6:1	MPC
				GB		100@ 5000		8.0:1	MPC

Engine Numbers	Transmission Type	Transmission Numbers	Chassis Numbers
W 0 000 001 - W 0 057 460	914/11	HA0000001 - HA0014826	470 29 00001 - 470 29 13312
640 0001 - 640 0889 640 3001 - 640 3013 640 4001 - 640 5781 (US & Can.) 640 7001 - 640 7012 (US & Can.)	914/01-5 spd 914/05-Sporto 914/01-5 spd 914/05-Sporto	750 0001 - 750 2668* 760 0001 - 760 0004*	914 04 30011 - 914 04 32668
W 0 057 461 - W 0 129 581	914/11	HA0014827 - HA0030093	471 29 00001 - 471 29 16231
641 0001 - 641 0268 641 3001 - 641 3030 641 4001 - 641 4163 (US & Can.) 641 7001 - 641 7015 (US & Can.)	914/01-5 spd 914/05-Sporto 914/01-5 spd 914/05-Sporto	751 0001 - 751 0443* 761 0001 - 761 0027*	914 14 30011 - 914 14 30443
W 0 129 582 - W 0 170 000	914/11	HA0030094 - HA0053072	472 29 01400 - 472 29 21580
EA 0000001 - EA 0057000	914/11		
642 0001 - 642 0269	914/01-5spd 914/05-Sporto	752 0001 - 0260* 762 0001 - *	914 24 30011 - 914 24 30260
632 5001 - 632 5026	915/20	915 R 005 - 915 R 045**	914 23 30011 - 914 23 30020 (Prototype 914 14 30195)
W 0 170 001 - W 0 250 000	914/12	HA0053072- HA0056362	473 29 00001 - 473 29 27660
EA 0057001 - EA 0098793		Numbering system was changed October 1, 1972 to the following format:	
EB 0000001 - EB 0009703		HA dd mm y	
		HA 01 10 2 - HA 31 12 2	
GA 0000001 - GA 0006765		and	
GB 0000001 - GB 0007401		HA 01 01 3 - HA 31 07 3	

Year Mfg.	Model Year	Official Model Design.	Engine Designation Official	Engine Designation Internal	Displ. cc.	Horse-power (DIN)-RPM	Stroke & Bore	Compr. Ratio	Fuel System Type
1973/ 1974	1974	914	1.8	EC	1795	76@ 4800	66/93	7.3:1	AFC
				AN		85@ 5000		8.6:1	Solex
			2.0	GA	1971	95@ 4900	71/94	7.6:1	MPC
				GB		100@ 5000		8.0:1	MPC
1974/ 1975	1975	914	1.8	EC	1795	76@ 4900	66/93	7.3:1	AFC
				AN		85@ 5000		8.6:1	Solex
			2.0	GB	1971	100@ 5000	71/94	8.0:1	MPC
				GC		88@ 4900		7.6:1	MPC
1975/ 1976	1976	914	1.8	EC	1795	76@ 4900	66/93	7.3:1	AFC
				AN		85@ 5000		8.6:1	Solex
			2.0	GB	1971	100@ 5000	71/94	8.0:1	MPC
				GC		88@ 4900		7.6:1	MPC

914-4 Engine Types

022	W	All Markets, 1.7
	EA	US/Canada 1972-1973, 1.7
	EB	California 1973, 1.7
	EC	US/Canada 1974-1976, 1.8
021	AN	RoW 1974-1976, 1.8 carbureted
039	GA	US/Canada 1973-1974, 2.0
	GB	RoW 1973-1976, 2.0
	GC	US/Canada 1975-1976, 2.0

Fuel System Types

MPC = Manifold Pressure Controlled
AFC = Air Flow Controlled

Engine Numbers	Transmission Type	Transmission Numbers	Chassis Numbers
EC 0000001 - EC 00037551	914/12	HA 01 08 3 - HA 31 12 3	474 29 00001 - 474 29 21379
		and	
AN 0000001 - AN 0008797	914/12	HA 01 01 4 - HA 31 07 4	
GA 0006766 - GA 00015021	914/12		
GB 0007402 - GB 0009821	914/12		
EC 0037552 - EC 0045072	914/12	HA 01 08 4 - HA 31 12 4	475 29 00001 - 475 29 11369
		and	
AN 0008798 - AN 0008898	914/12	HA 01 01 5 - HA 31 07 5	
GB 0009822 - GB 0010778	914/12		
GC 0000001 - GC 0002914	914/12		
EC 0045073 - *	914/12	HA 01 08 5 - HA 31 12 5	476 29 00001 - 476 29 04100
		and	
AN 0008899 - *	914/12	HA 01 01 6 - HA 31 07 6*	
GB 0010779 - *	914/12		
GC 0002915 - GC 0006946	914/12		

** ending numbers are not known in these sequences*

** ending numbers are not known in these sequences*

*** the prototype 916 was originally fitted with the 914/01 transmission*

Total Production

914-4	115,596
914-6	3,340
916	11

Spotter's Guide

FRONT

1970
Painted bumpers, standard
Chrome bumpers, optional
Optional Hella fog lights, US
Optional Hella fog or driving lights, non-US (yellow France)
Amber turn signal lens, US
Clear turn signal lens, Italy
Clear/amber turn signal lens except US and Italy
Black rubber bumper cap
Black lower valance
White plastic headlight surround
Chrome headlight retaining ring
Aluminum capped washer jets

1973
Matte black bumper, standard
Rubber bumper guards, US

1974
Optional color coordinated front spoiler on *Limited Edition*
Optional black front spoiler other models
Optional headlight washer nozzles on bumper cap (Sweden)
Black windshield washer nozzles, from # 474 290 2454
Black headlight surrounds

1975
Revised front bumper replaces bumper and bumper cap
Bumper guards for California and Maryland
Optional rectangular Bosch fog lights, US
Optional rectangular Bosch fog or driving lights, non-US (yellow for France)
Black headlight retaining ring
Revised headlight washer nozzles (Sweden)

1970 914-6 Euro spec.

1971 914-4

1973 US Spec.

1976 2.0

SIDE

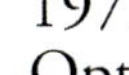

1970
Reflector on front fender, US
Side marker on front fender, Denmark, Italy
Matte black rocker panels
Painted roof pillars, standard
Vinyl covered roof pillars with aluminum trim, optional
Optional *positive* side stripes
Painted steel 4½ x 15" four lug wheels, 914-4
Painted steel 5½ x 15" five lug wheels, 914-6 (chrome optional)
Optional forged Fuchs alloy 5½ x 14", wheels, 914-6
Optional cast Mahle alloy 5½ x 15", wheels, 914-6
Chrome hub caps without emblem, 914-4, US
Chrome hub caps with VW emblem, 914-4, non-US
Stainless steel hubcaps with dull finish or enameled Porsche crests, 914-6 with steel wheels
Optional Pedrini 5½ x 15" wheels, 914-4

1971
Optional painted 5½ x 15" steel wheels

1972
Revised longer side mirror

1973
Optional Pedrini 5½ x 15" wheels
Optional Fuchs 5½ x 15" wheels
Optional Mahle 5½ x 15" wheels

1974
Painted rocker panels on *Limited Edition*
Negative side stripes, optional
5½ x 15" steel sport wheels without hubcaps, standard
Pedrini wheels not available
Vinyl covered roof pillars, standard

1970 914-6

1971 914-4

1973 US spec. 2.0

1973 Euro spec. 2.0

1974 Limited Edition

1976 2.0

REAR

1970
Painted bumpers, standard
Chrome bumpers, optional
Gold P-O-R-S-C-H-E letters on engine lid, US
Tail light unit with red turn signal, US
Tail light unit with amber turn signal, not US or France
Tail light unit with yellow back up light, France
Gold 914 or 914-6 script on tail panel, US
Gold 914 VW Porsche or 914-6
VW Porsche script on tail panel, not US
Black rubber bumper cap
Black lower valance (4 and 6 were different) with hole

1972 (late)
Short rear valance on 914-4

1973
Black metal 914, 2.0 and 1.7 scripts on tail, US
Black 914 VW Porsche script on tail, not US

1973 continued
Matte black bumper, standard
Silver P-O-R-S-C-H-E letters on engine lid, US

1974
Black plastic 914, 2.0 and 1.8 scripts on tail panel, US
Rubber bumper guards, US
Optional color coordinated rear valance on *Limited Edition*
Plastic chrome P-O-R-S-C-H-E letters on engine lid, US

1975
Revised rear bumper replaces bumper and bumper cap
Revised license lights
Bumper guards for California and Maryland

1976
Black vinyl 914 and 2.0 decals on tail panel, US

Euro spec. 1970 914-6

1973 US spec. 2.0

1974 Can Am Limited Edition 2.0

1976 2.0

INTERIOR

1970
Silver buttons in center of instruments
Ignition switch on dash, 914-6
Ignition switch on column, 914-4
Wiper switch on column, 914-6
Wiper switch on dash, 914-4
Hard rubber rimmed steering wheel, standard
Leather rimmed steering wheel, optional
Porsche crest on horn pad, all 914-6 and US 914-4
Wolfsburg crest on horn pad, 914-4, not US
Fixed passenger's seat
Tethered foot rest
Optional small central console deposit
Hand throttle lever on floor in front of shift lever, 914-6
Optional pad between seats
Chrome and black window crank
Aluminum threshold plates

1971
Smooth grained vinyl on seats/door panels

1972
HAZARD on 4-way knob
Wiper switch on column, 914-4
Larger glove compartment knob
Revised rubber & leather steering wheels
Larger rear view mirror
Moveable passenger's seat
Flattened heat control knob with *ON/OFF* US
Seat belt retractors added January
Basket weave material on door panels
Left and right vents on dashboard
Words added to blower control

1970-1971 early seating arrangement

1973
Optional center console with three gauges
Storage compartment between seats, optional
Illuminated defrost warning light, US
Round heat knob, mid-year
Non-collapsing parking brake
Black inner door handle surround June/July
All black window crank June/July
Black plastic threshold plates, from #473 291 8919

1974
Smaller red scale on oil temperature gauge in center console
Headlight washer switch to upper left of blower control, Sweden
Seat belt warning light, US
Leatherette rimmed steering wheel, optional
Black center buttons on instruments mid-year

1975
Domed ignition switch
Tartan cloth seat inserts, optional
Black surround on blower control
Fat window cranks
Wide basket-weave vinyl

1970 914-6 dashboard area

1973 2.0 with VPC air-conditioning

Exterior Colors

Nearly all cars produced by Porsche after the 1955 model year were finished in enamel paint, which was baked following application. An exception to this involved the metallic paints used from 1966 through 1969, which were lacquer. Some early silver 914s may have this lacquer finish. Note there was a paint number difference between this metallic lacquer and the so-called *two-coat process* enamel paint, which replaced it in 1970.

The plate bearing the paint number, indicating the original color of the car, is on the left door hinge post. The numbers used are the ones found in the *Code* column of the following chart. From 1970 through 1972, the order number (*Number* column) was the same for 914s and 911s. A number ending in *10* signified Targa for 911s and since all 914s were kind of like Targas, they used the same number. After 1972, the numbering changed to a Volkswagen system and most colors were shared with contemporary Volkswagens rather than Porsches.

One final note; the colors followed by an asterisk (*) are those that were available at extra cost, i.e., metallics and black. Custom paint color (paint to sample) was always an option ($136.50 in 1971).

1970: 914, some 914-6

Color	Number	Code
Tangerine (Blood Orange)	2310	L 21 E
Metallic Red*	8110	L 97 D
Canary Yellow	2910	L 11 E
Signal Orange	1410	L 20 E
Light Ivory	1110	L 80 E
Irish (Forest) Green	1510	L 60 E
Metallic Green*	8310	L 97 P
Metallic Blue*	8410	L 98 P
Adriatic Blue	1610	L 50 E
Silver Metallic (2-coat)*	8010	L 96 D
Gemini Blue*	8610	L 96 E

1970: some 914-6

Color	Number	Code
Tangerine (Blood Orange)	2310	018
Metallic Red*	8110	021
Canary Yellow	2910	115
Signal Orange	1410	116
Light Ivory	1110	131
Irish (Forest) Green	1510	213
Metallic Green*	8310	221
Metallic Blue*	8410	324
Adriatic Blue	1610	327
Silver Metallic (2-coat)*	8010	925
Gemini Blue*	8610	330

1971: 914, some 914-6

Color	Number	Code
Tangerine (Blood Orange)	2310	L 21 E
Bahia Red	1310	L 30 E
Canary Yellow	2910	L 11 E
Signal Orange	1410	L 20 E
Light Ivory	1110	L 80 E
Irish (Forest) Green	1510	L 60 E
Willow Green	4310	L 63 K
Gemini Blue*	8610	L 96 E
Adriatic Blue	1610	L 50 E
Black*	1010	L 04 I
Silver Metallic (2-coat)*	8010	L 96 D
Gold Metallic*	8810	L 97 G

1971: some 914-6

Color	Number	Code
Tangerine (Blood Orange)	2310	018
Bahia Red	1310	022
Canary Yellow	2910	115
Signal Orange	1410	116
Light Ivory	1110	131
Irish (Forest) Green	1510	213
Willow Green	4310	223
Gemini Blue*	8610	330
Adriatic Blue	1610	327
Black*	1010	700
Silver Metallic (2-coat)*	8010	925
Gold Metallic*	8810	133

1972:

Color	Number	Code
Saturn (Chrome) Yellow	2610	L 13 M
Signal Orange	1410	L 20 E
Tangerine (Blood Orange)	2310	L 21 E
Bahia Red	1310	L 30 E
Black*	1010	L 04 I
Adriatic Blue	1610	L 50 E
Irish (Forest) Green	1510	L 60 E
Willow Green	4310	L 63 K
Light Ivory	1110	L 80 E
Silver Metallic*	8010	L 96 D
Gemini Blue*	8610	L 96 E
Gold Metallic*	8810	L 97 G

1973:

Color	Number	Code
Light Ivory	B8V9	L 80 E
Bahia Red	G2V9	L 30 E
Olympic Blue	J8V9	L 51 P
Saturn (Chrome) Yellow	B2V9	L 13 M
Phoenix (Rallye) Red	G5V9	L 32 K
Ravenna Green	M5V9	L 65 K
Zambezi Green	M7V9	L 64 K
Sunflower (Summer)Yellow	B3V9	L 13 K
Signal Orange	E2V9	L 20 E
Black*	A1V9	L 04 I
Delphi Green Metallic*	W1V9	L 99 A
Marathon Blue Metallic*	X2V9	L 96 M
Alaska Blue Metallic*	X4V9	L 96 B
Silver Metallic*	Z2V9	L 96 D

1974:

Color	Number	Code
Light Ivory	B8V9	L 80 E
Bahia Red	G2V9	L 30 E
Signal Orange	E2V9	L 20 E
Sunflower (Summer)Yellow	B3V9	L 13 K
Ravenna Green	M5V9	L 65 K
Olympic Blue	J8V9	L 51 P
Phoenix Red	G5V9	L 32 K
Zambezi Green	M7V9	L 64 K
Saturn Yellow	B2V9	L 13 M
Black*	A1V9	L 04 I
Delphi Green Metallic*	W1V9	L 99 A
Marathon Blue Metallic*	X2V9	L 96 M
Alaska Blue Metallic*	X4V9	L 96 B
Silver Metallic*	Z2V9	L 96 D

1975:

Color	Number	Code
Berber Yellow	B5 V9	L 11 D
Sunflower (Summer)Yellow	B3 V9	L 13 K
Nepal Orange	E5 V9	L 20 C
Malaga Red	H5 V9	L 30 C
Scarlet (Mars) Red	H3 V9	L 31 M
Black*	A1 V9	L 04 I
Lagoon Blue	J1 V9	L 50 C
Forest Green	M7 V9	L 64 K
Light Ivory	B8 V9	L 80 E
Palma Metallic*	Y1 V9	L 95 K
Silver Metallic*	Z4 V9	L 96 D
Ancona Metallic*	X5 V9	L 97 B
Copper Metallic*	W2 V9	L 99 K
Viper Green Metallic*	Y5 V9	L 96 N

1976:

Color	Number	Code
Sunflower (Summer)Yellow	B3 V9	L 13 K
Nepal Orange	E5 V9	L 20 C
Malaga Red	H5 V9	L 30 C
Scarlet (Mars) Red	H3 V9	L 31 M
Black*	A1 V9	L 04 I
Lagoon Blue	J1 V9	L 50 C
Light Ivory	B8 V9	L 80 E
Viper Green Metallic*	Y5 V9	L 96 N
Silver Metallic*	Z4 V9	L 96 D
Ancona Metallic*	X5 V9	L 97 B

Option Packages

Appearance Group

1970-1972
Vinyl-covered roll bar w/ anodized aluminum trim
Dual horns
Chrome bumpers
Fog lights
5½ x 15" Pedrini wheels (optional)
165/15 tires
Leather-covered steering wheel & shift boot
Pile carpet

1973
Vinyl-covered roll bar w/ anodized aluminum trim
Dual horns
Chrome bumpers
Fog lights
Pedrini (optional 1.7) or Fuchs (2.0) alloy wheels
Front and rear anti-sway bars (2.0)
Leather-covered steering wheel & shift boot
Pile carpet
Center console with center armrest and storage compartment (2.0)

1974-1976
Dual horns
Fog lights
Leatherette-covered steering wheel
Center armrest with storage compartment
Leather shift boot

Limited Edition (Can-AM) 1974

Can Am equipment included black/yellow or white/orange paint scheme, center console, front and rear sway bars, rear anodized roll bar trim, painted Mahle wheels, dual horns, leatherette steering wheel, driving lights and color coordinated bumpers, side stripes, rocker panels and front spoiler.

Interior Colors and Materials

1970: Color	Number
Vinyl, Seats, Door Panels	
Brown	400
Tan	500
Black	700
Basket-weave Vinyl, Seat Inserts	
Brown	400
Tan	500
Black	700
Leather, Seats, Door Panels (914-6 only)	
Brown	402
Tan	501
Black	700
Leather, Seat Inserts (914-6 only)	
Brown	403
Tan	502
Black	701
Corduroy, Seat Inserts	
Brown	411
Tan	503
Black	709
Hound's Tooth Cloth, Seat Inserts	
Black/tan/white	430
Black/white	730
Carpet - Loop	
Brown	401
Tan	501
Charcoal	700
Carpet - Felt	
Brown	401
Tan	501
Charcoal	700

1971: Color	Number
Vinyl, Seats, Door Panels	
Brown	401
Tan	501
Black	701
Basket-weave Vinyl, Seat Inserts	
Brown	401
Tan	501
Black	701
Leather, Seats, Door Panels (914-6 only)	
Brown	402
Tan	501
Black	700
Leather, Seat Inserts (914-6 only)	
Brown	403
Tan	502
Black	701
Corduroy, Seat Inserts	
Brown	400
Tan	500
Black	700
Carpet - Loop	
Brown	402
Tan	501
Charcoal	701
Carpet - Felt	
Brown	402
Tan	501
Charcoal	700

1972: Color	Number
Vinyl, Seats	
Brown	402
Tan	502
Black	702
Basket-weave Vinyl, Seat Inserts, Door Panels	
Brown	401
Tan	501
Black	701
Corduroy, Seat Inserts	
Brown	400
Tan	500
Black	700
Carpet - Loop	
Brown	402
Tan	501
Charcoal	701
Carpet - Felt	
Brown	402
Tan	501
Charcoal	700

1973: Color	Number
Vinyl, Seats	
Brown	402
Tan	502
Black	702
Basket-weave Vinyl, Seat Inserts, Door Panels	
Brown	401
Tan	501
Black	701
Corduroy, Seat Inserts	
Brown	400
Tan	500
Black	700

Carpet - Loop

Brown	402
Tan	501
Charcoal	701

Carpet - Felt

Brown	402
Tan	501
Charcoal	700

1974: Color	Number
Vinyl, Seats	
Brown	402
Tan	502
Black	702
Basket-weave Vinyl, Seat Inserts, Door Panels	
Brown	401
Tan	501
Black	701
Corduroy, Seat Inserts	
Brown	400
Tan	500
Black	700
Carpet - Loop	
Brown	402
Dark Tan	503
Tan	504
Charcoal	701
Carpet - Felt	
Brown	402
Tan	501
Charcoal	700

1975: Color	Number
Vinyl, Seats	
Black	713
Buckskin	413
White	513
Basket-weave Vinyl, Seat Inserts, Door Panels (New Design)	
Black	713
Buckskin	413
White	513
Corduroy, Seat Inserts, (Wide Rib)	
Black	705
Buckskin	405
White	505
Tartan Cloth, Seat Inserts (All with black vinyl)	
Yellow	BN 1
Green	BN 2
Greenish-Yellow	BN 3
Orange	BN 4
Bright-Red	BN 5
Burgundy-Red	BN 6
Ski-Blue	BN 7
Matisse-Blue	BN 8
Black/Charcoal	BN 9
Carpet - Pile	
Charcoal	706
Tan	406
Oatmeal	506
Carpet - Felt	
Charcoal	705
Tan	405

1976: Color	Number
Vinyl, Seats	
Black	713
Tan	413
White	513
Basket-weave Vinyl, Seat Inserts, Door Panels (New Design)	
Black	713
Tan	413
White	513
Corduroy, Seat Inserts, (Wide Rib)	
Black	705
Tan	405
White	505
Tartan Cloth, Seat Inserts (All with black vinyl)	
Yellow	BN 1
Green	CB 6
Orange	BN 4
Bright-Red	BN 5
Burgundy-Red	BN 6
Black/Charcoal	BN 9
Blue	CB 7
Carpet - Pile	
Charcoal	706
Tan	406
Oatmeal	506
Carpet - Felt	
Charcoal	705
Tan	405

Index

H

I

J

K

L

M

N

O

P

Q

R

S

T

U

V

W